TRICIA GUILD
DECORATING WITH COLOUR

SPECIAL PHOTOGRAPHY BY DAVID MONTGOMERY

TEXT BY TRICIA GUILD WITH ELIZABETH WILHIDE

conran
OCTOPUS

For L.G. and R.P.... and his yellow

AUTHOR'S ACKNOWLEDGEMENTS
I would like to thank the following people who have contributed to this book:
David Montgomery for the quality of his light, Jeremy Hilder for helping him;
Jo Willer for her keen eye, constant support and encouragement;
Simon Jeffreys, Virginia Bruce, Lisa Guild, Nim Thompson and the team at Designers Guild;
Evelyn Shearer; from Conran Octopus Anne Furniss, Jo Bradshaw, Liz Wilhide, Jessica Walton,
Julia Golding and Meryl Lloyd for her patience and brilliant art direction.

Project Editor JOANNA BRADSHAW

Art Editor MERYL LLOYD

Picture Research JESSICA WALTON

Production JULIA GOLDING

First published in 1992 under the title of Tricia Guild on Colour
by Conran Octopus Limited
a part of Octopus Publishing Group
2–4 Heron Quays, London, E14 4JP
www.conran-octopus.co.uk

This paperback edition published in 1995 by Conran Octopus Limited
Reprinted 1995, 1996, 1997, 2001, 2002

British Library Cataloguing-in-Publication Data
A catalogue record for this book is available from the British Library
ISBN 1 84091 264 2

Typeset by Hunters Armley Ltd.
Printed and bound in China

For details of Designers Guild fabrics featured in this book, please refer
to the fabric directory on page 186.

C O N T E N T S

FOREWORD 6

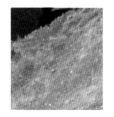

A SENSE OF COLOUR
10

WHITE
32

BLUE
46

GREEN
72

YELLOW
94

NATURAL
118

TERRACOTTA
132

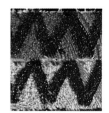

RED
150

COLOUR PALETTES
170

FOREWORD

'WHEN I CHOOSE A COLOUR IT IS NOT BECAUSE OF ANY
SCIENTIFIC THEORY. IT COMES FROM OBSERVATION,
FROM FEELING, FROM THE INNERMOST NATURE OF
THE EXPERIENCE IN QUESTION.'

HENRI MATISSE

My life and work have been deeply influenced by colour
and its potential. This book is a celebration, a way of sharing
my involvement with colour and the way it enhances
and enriches so many aspects of life.
It is the ultimate expression of vitality.

Tricia Guild

A SENSE OF COLOUR

'SPRING IS TENDER, GREEN YOUNG CORN AND
PINK APPLE BLOSSOMS.
AUTUMN IS THE CONTRAST OF THE YELLOW LEAVES
AGAINST VIOLET TONES.
WINTER IS THE SNOW WITH BLACK SILHOUETTES.
BUT NOW, IF SUMMER IS THE OPPOSITION OF BLUES
AGAINST AN ELEMENT OF ORANGE, IN THE GOLD BRONZE
OF THE CORN, ONE COULD PAINT A PICTURE WHICH
EXPRESSED THE MOOD OF THE SEASONS IN EACH OF THE
CONTRASTS OF THE COMPLEMENTARY COLOURS . . .'

LETTER TO HIS BROTHER THEO,

VINCENT VAN GOGH

LIVING WITH COLOUR

COLOUR HAS THE POWER TO TRANSFORM THE SMALLEST OF SPACES INTO A VITAL AND UPLIFTING ENVIRONMENT.

We are fortunate to be living at a time when colour is available to everyone. Colour printing, colour photography, colour television, are all relatively recent developments, and through these technological advances we are able now to acquire an entire visual education without even leaving the living room. Such constant exposure to colourful imagery was simply not available to our forebears, even two generations ago.

In decoration, too, colours of every conceivable hue are achievable and affordable — in wallpaper, paint, fabric, carpet and ceramic tile, so it has become easier than ever before to use colour and to 'live' colour. An extraordinarily powerful subject and a fascinating tool, colour can alter a domestic environment, enhancing the mood of an interior and improving the quality of life within.

Despite this new accessibility, many people are still remarkably hesitant when it comes to applying colour in their own homes. There is a tendency to cling to stale colour schemes which offer safe solutions and to opt for muddy non-colours rather than positive tones.

One reason for this hesitancy may be the dominance of the plain white wall in contemporary decoration, a legacy of 'modern' movements in interior design and architecture resulting in a minimalism which has only recently been challenged. Another reason for present-day reticence in the use of colour could well be that the instinctive handling of vivid colour and rich pattern, skills which our ancestors enjoyed in previous centuries, has been lost. Despite a really rather limited range of colours, Georgian, Regency and Victorian rooms were often surprisingly expressive and exuberant, proving that colour can be uniquely uplifting, lending energy and life to an interior.

Perhaps the sheer breadth of choice available today is confusing, not to say intimidating. Easy, coordinated ranges of fabric and paint help the nervous decorator assemble a coherent scheme, but this is at the cost of a great deal of vitality and creativity. Some people imagine that colour is tiring

LIVING WITH COLOUR

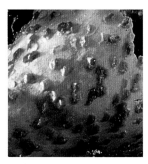

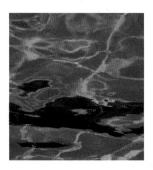

to live with, forgetting how dreary it is to sit in dull rooms without a spark of interest to stimulate the eye. Others think that colour is more appropriate in hot countries, where the light is strong. But cheerfulness is not the sole preserve of the sunny South: one has only to look at Scandinavian folk art and decoration to see strong vivid greens and tomato reds used to banish the misery of long, grey winter days.

The ability of colour to transform surroundings, to excite a variety of reactions, to uplift and inspire is second to none. Our responses to it lie deep, almost defying analysis or explanation. Colour speaks directly, with an appeal that is almost visceral. It can influence powerfully by association, through common uses embedded in culture, or by calling up personal experiences locked in the memory. Since civilization began, colour has been one of the principal ways in which we express our creativity and *joie de vivre*. No matter how dormant or under-used, colour sense can be brought back to life and encouraged to blossom. It starts with observation. Few people are born with an instinctive sense of colour; more often than not it has to be learned like any other skill. The eye is an incredibly sensitive organ which is capable of making millions of subtle colour distinctions, so to ignore this potential depth of response would be like eating the same food every day.

One way of becoming acquainted with colour is to build up a scrapbook of favourite colour swatches, scraps of fabric, ribbon, postcards, photographs – anything that inspires you. Many people find they are attracted naturally to a certain family of colours – rich earth colours, or a variety of blues for example. Others are drawn exclusively to a particular shade for a time, until a new colour takes their fancy. Some women can become sensitized to a specific colour during pregnancy, just as others have cravings for certain foods. This phenomenon appears in Nicholson Baker's novel *Room Temperature*, where the narrator describes his wife's obsession with cranberry red.

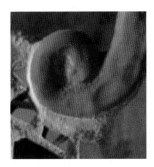

Colour is so much a part of our lives and even our way of thinking that many people (myself included) unconsciously assign different colours to letters, numbers or even sounds. For example, I have, since early childhood, experienced days of the week as particular colours: Monday is pale blue; Thursday is lime green; Friday is brown; Sunday is pink.

'Colours are the mother tongue of the subconscious,' said Jung and it is obvious from the central role that colour has played in folklore and religions over many centuries, as well as its innumerable everyday associations, that colour operates on many levels. Nearly every colour at one time or in one culture or another has had spiritual connotations: colour is literally magic. On a more prosaic level, the vast sums of money spent by advertising agencies deciding which colour will appeal most to the high street consumer, testify to the powerful way in which colour communicates values and feelings. Colours often remind people of something else, sometimes from way back in their past.

From appreciating colours in all their richness and diversity, it is a short step to the endlessly fascinating exploration of colour combinations. The electric mixtures, where the colours sing, the compatible families, where each colour supports the others, and the simple graphic contrasts, all have an important role to play in decoration.

Colour is subjective. But despite the individual nature of our reactions and responses, it is important to look at how colour works – in theory and in practice, in nature, art and in science – before considering ways of using it successfully in our own surroundings.

THE NATURE OF COLOUR

THE FRESH NEW GREEN OF BALINESE PADDY FIELDS SHOWS HOW NATURE CAN PROVIDE THE MOST BRILLIANT COLOUR OF ALL.

The names people use to describe different colours can be very revealing. Leaf green, fuchsia, buttercup yellow, midnight blue, rose, nut brown, all conjure up the world of nature. It is not surprising that nature is one of the most rewarding sources of inspiration for those looking to extend their colour vocabulary. Colour begins with nature. And nature is what all our subjective colour memories and responses ultimately have in common. Green is calming and restful because it is reminiscent of green fields, fresh new growth and the landscape. Blue is expansive, airy and watery like the sky and the sea. Yellow is warming and positive like the golden sun. Red is nature's accent – a danger signal, as in bright poisonous berries or deadly fungi, or the eye-catching attraction of a coxcomb or display of feathers. The colours of childhood places, of gardens and flowers are impressions that very often stay with us for ever.

Sometimes nature close at hand is just too familiar to stimulate the imagination, which is why travel can be so reviving. The experience of seeing new landscapes under different conditions of light can change our whole perception of colour. And after time away, we often see the colours in our own landscape with fresh eyes. Seasonal change can give much the same refreshing contrast.

Nature is not only a source of colour ideas, it can also provide the colours themselves in the form of natural dyes and pigments. The oldest colours of all come from the earth, such as ochre and umber from clay, while colours obtained from animals and vegetables include madder, indigo and cochineal (from crushed beetles). The art of using natural dyes was almost obliterated by the Industrial Revolution but William Morris revived the technique when he experimented and perfected the use of natural colours in his printed fabrics. Compare a Morris pattern using natural dyes with a nineteenth-century equivalent created with the harsh chemical dyes of the period, and the difference in subtlety and colour balance is obvious.

THE ART OF COLOUR

While the colour names we owe to nature may be beautifully evocative, for sheer precision it is hard to beat descriptions such as crimson, viridian, vermilion, burnt sienna, ultramarine and cerulean blue. The terminology associated with artists' colours is rich and exact, making fine distinctions between different shades. We even see some colours through an artist's eyes. Titian red, for example, is a descriptive term that has passed into everyday usage as a result of the strikingly original tones achieved by this Italian Renaissance painter.

Nowhere has colour been studied more intensely, its characteristics and potential explored more thoroughly than in the work of artists – from Piero della Francesca, Bellini and Vermeer to Monet, Van Gogh, Matisse and Kandinsky. All artists necessarily have been concerned with colour, some have been obsessed by it. Powerful insights into the use of colour and the feelings and moods it can inspire can be found in a wide variety of artists' work: the jewel-like intensity of medieval paintings, where colour has its own iconography; the delicate fresco colours of a Giotto or a Botticelli, the luminous tonalities of Piero della Francesca, as well as Titian, Vermeer and, of course, Turner, with his elemental vision of light and colour.

Closer to our time, particularly after the scientific nature of colour began to be understood, colour itself became the subject rather than an aspect of composition or an adjunct of naturalism. The paintings of the Impressionists show a passionate desire to record what the artist really saw at a particular moment, to be true to perception. In this they were responding directly to nineteenth-century advances in optics. Light was broken up into bright patches, dots, flecks and brushstrokes of colour, a fluid and sometimes dazzling palette which vibrated on the eye. Monet's series of paintings of Rouen cathedral or his late studies of water-lilies are powerful exercises in pure light and pure colour, while Seurat's pictures are composed entirely of tiny points of colour, to be blended in the eye of the beholder.

THE ART OF COLOUR

'HARVEST' BY
KAFFE FASSETT.

'WATERLEAF' BY
JANICE TCHALENKO.

If the colours of nature and light preoccupied the Impressionists, colour later began to be used in a very different way by other artists: symbolically as in Gauguin's paintings of the South Seas, or to conjure up a mood, as in the influential work of Whistler. A joy in juxtaposing brilliant expressive colours is evident in the distinctive paintings of Van Gogh. He thought and wrote a great deal about colour, believing the artist of the future would be 'a colourist such as has never yet been' and characterized his own work as 'the search for the high yellow note'. Cézanne, rejecting the subjective basis of Impressionism, also used colour in an entirely new sense, as a way of expressing what he thought was eternal or essential in the scene before him. The late Impressionists, Bonnard and Vuillard, painted intimate studies of nineteenth-century interiors, steeped in colour and dancing with pattern.

By the twentieth century, colour was no longer tied to nature, but came from inner feeling, an approach which found its fullest expression with Matisse. His characteristic palette of blue-green, brilliant blue and deep red was the signature of his creative personality. Matisse's paintings rely on colour relationships for their structure and they remain a boundless source of ideas and inspiration for me. Similarly, the often shocking colour combinations of the Expressionists such as Kirchner, Nölde and Munch display profound feeling and intensity.

Delaunay was another artist working in the early twentieth century who gave absolute priority to colour. 'Colour alone is both form and subject' he believed; many of his paintings were essays in colour where the subject is almost dissolved. Nature was no longer represented in form or motif but in the pure abstract colour relationships. Picasso – perhaps the archetypal twentieth-century artist – progressed from the early Blue and Rose periods characterized by a single defining shade, to the protean colour energies of Cubism and beyond.

The Bauhaus, the avant-garde school of modernist art, design and

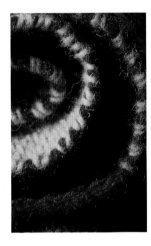

'LARGE FLOWER' BY
HOWARD HODGKIN.

WOOLLEN THROW BY
RICHARD WOMERSLEY.

architecture which flourished in Germany between the two World Wars, ran courses on colour theory taught by Klee and Kandinsky. Their fascinating attempt to come up with a universal visual language related basic forms such as the circle, square and triangle to primary colours, and assigned particular qualities and even sounds to each of the colours in the spectrum.

Past or present, art in all its forms provides new ways of seeing and experiencing colour. I have been personally influenced by many painters, from Mark Rothko to David Bomberg. Living artists whose work I find particularly inspiring for their use of colour include Frank Auerbach and Howard Hodgkin. Part of my philosophy at Designers Guild is to work with contemporary artists and I have commissioned both Howard Hodgkin and, more recently, Michael Heindorff to design textiles for our collections.

Broadening the field from fine art to the decorative arts in general, colour is no less a vital element in other areas of creative endeavour, from needlepoint and weaving to ceramics. One of my longest associations with a contemporary craftsman has been with Kaffe Fassett, whose colour sense and use of texture in his painterly needlepoints has inspired a whole new generation to experiment with colour. The weaver Richard Womersley has also long been associated with Designers Guild. Ceramics are a particular passion, both collecting and working with celebrated ceramicists such as Janice Tchalenko, Carol McNichol and Liz Hodges.

While nature takes us back to basics, art can be a medium for heightening awareness, relating colour directly to the expression of feelings and ideas.

THE SCIENCE OF COLOUR

Colour, in a scientific sense, is how we perceive waves of light. Colour is not a quality of an object, it does not reside in anything: in other words, there is no 'red' in red shoes. When light strikes an object, the object absorbs all the wavelengths of light except what we see reflected back at us: red shoes, for example, absorb all the wavelengths of light, except the red ones, and this is why we see the shoes as red.

Since Newton we have known that white light when broken up by a prism – or waterdrops as in a rainbow – reveals a continuous spectrum of colour, from the longest red wavelengths to the shortest, which are blue. For the sake of convenience, the spectrum is usually represented as six distinct bands of red, orange, yellow, green, blue and violet. In a colour wheel, the ends of the spectrum are brought round to join in a circle.

Although the colour wheel is something of an abstract construction, it is useful in helping to understand the effect colours have on each other. Artists such as Van Gogh made deliberate use of the notion of complementary colours in the composition of paintings. (My own response to and use of colour is more instinctive, less analytical – and I am a little wary of subjecting what feels essentially personal to scientific analysis!).

At its most simplified, the colour wheel consists of the three 'primary' colours red, yellow and blue, the three 'secondary' colours orange, green and violet and three 'tertiary' colours – such as turquoise – which are the colours resulting from equal mixtures of a primary and a secondary. Just as mixing all the colours in the spectrum produces white light, mixing all three primaries would have the same effect.

The colour wheel shows true colour relationships very clearly. Colours which sit opposite one another are contrasting or 'complementary'. Complementary pairs – red and green, yellow and violet, orange and blue – if mixed together as coloured light, would give white light. Side by side they appear to vibrate, offering exciting decorative possibilities.

MAKING COLOUR WORK

Colour theory may appear to have little relevance when it comes down to the practical issues of choosing curtain fabric or paint, but a fundamental appreciation of how colour works really can help, especially when you are trying to compose a colour scheme using more than a couple of colours or variations of one basic shade. Knowing which colours fall into a family that harmonizes naturally, which 'vibrate' and why some combinations don't work at all can be of enormous assistance and help to create a vibrant, exciting and original colour scheme.

'STILL LIFE' BY MICHAEL HEINDORFF, A PAINTING REPRODUCED AS A FABRIC BY DESIGNERS GUILD.

Quite fine adjustments can make all the difference. This was underlined for me recently while we were in the process of printing a fabric designed by the artist Michael Heindorff. The print was a complex pattern requiring 21 different screens; as the first sample came off the machines, something looked wrong. The colour of the flowers in the original artwork – a particular shade of red – had not been captured and the image lacked life. With machines running and printers waiting anxiously, I hurriedly scoured a colour atlas and eventually found the perfect shade. The change was extraordinary – the balance, light and quality of the original painting was restored by an infinitesimal alteration in tone.

In a similar way you can use variables of colour tone and saturation to help understand how to put together different combinations. Colours that work in harmony together, such as lighter or darker shades of the same colour are naturally comfortable to the eye, while more exciting and dynamic combinations make use of a pair of complementary but 'opposite' colours such as red and green. By using a fraction of a complementary colour as a sharp accent you can set up more vibrant effects, perhaps offset by an intermediary shade.

Successful colour combinations often depend on getting the proportions right. A touch of contrasting colour is lively and refreshing; too much can be uncomfortable if blocks of vibrating colour are competing for attention.

COLOUR IN DECORATION

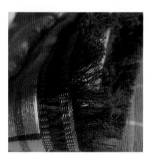

Whether we know it or not, we are subtly influenced by the way colour has been used over the centuries in the interior. People have always sought to surround themselves with colour and established traditions still affect our ways of using colour today.

It is extremely difficult to be accurate about the precise colours that were used in the interiors of old houses and buildings. A subject of considerable academic study and scientific analysis, the history of colour is continually being revized as new discoveries are made. Outside this academic sphere it is hard to imagine how rooms in historic houses really looked under lighting conditions vastly different from our own and before years of wear and tear had aged them beyond recognition.

Until the nineteenth century the range of colours available for practical use was much more limited than today. Most paints were derived from earth pigments, while fabrics were printed with muted vegetable dyes: this gave a serviceable palette of off-white, grey, buff, terracotta, red, green, brown and black. Really pure, intense colours tended to be rare and expensive. Pure blue, derived from the costly mineral lapis lazuli, seldom featured on a large scale, although Prussian blue dates from the eighteenth century.

During the eighteenth century, the colours used to decorate domestic interiors often had a natural association with a particular material. Doors and woodwork were typically brown, for example; plastered walls, especially in halls and service rooms might have been a pale stone colour. Green was fashionable for painted panelling for a large part of the century while dining rooms in affluent households might have been hung with red damask – red has long been associated with eating rooms and other places where there was an element of theatre and display.

A much lighter touch came in with the Rococo thanks (in part) to Madame de Pompadour's preference for pastels. Pink, pale yellow, light green and powder blue were fashionable until the turn of the century. Our

contemporary convention of decorating bedrooms in light, pastel shades owes something to the elegance of the eighteenth-century French boudoir.

At the end of the century tastes changed and the brilliant colours of neoclassicism came to the fore. Regency and Empire rooms were often highly coloured and the advances in synthetic pigments at this time meant that bright colour was easier to achieve than ever before. The first stable bright yellow came in the 1820s with the development of chrome yellow. Neoclassical schemes, based on archaeological finds at Pompeii and elsewhere, saw rooms decorated in rich reds, yellow, lilac and a particular shade of green, which, ever since that period, has been associated with Robert Adam, who used it in his architectural painting schemes.

Most of us are familiar with the Victorian palette and its rich and sombre combinations of magenta, maroon, brown, deep blue and olive green. A revolution in colour occurred mid-century, when the discovery of synthetic dyes vastly expanded the range of affordable colours. These new shades were frankly garish compared to the old earth- or vegetable-based colours: new colours included bright pink, mauve and magenta, named after a Crimean battle. Victorian rooms were multi-coloured and multi-patterned, often quite stifling to modern eyes.

By the late nineteenth century, a reaction to the dull, deep Victorian colours was inevitable. The 'greenery-yallery' of the Aesthetics, a colour which swept through furnishings and fashion, together with the Arts and Crafts revival of vegetable colour, marked a turning point in the use of colour in the home.

The twentieth century saw the introduction of the first brilliant white paint when titanium white appeared in the 1920s. After this time, white was suddenly no longer a mean, utility colour but the height of sophistication in the hands of fashionable society decorators such as Syrie Maugham. Later, white became the symbol of architectural purity and white walls an essential feature of modernist, minimalist rooms.

COLOUR AND CULTURE

VIVID ARCHITECTURAL DETAIL FROM AROUND THE WORLD – HAITI, MOROCCO AND UZBEKISTAN.

Nowadays, thanks to great strides in the technology of fabric printing and paint manufacture, we take for granted a vast range of colours in decoration – paints that are safe (lead-free), easy to use and widely available – a breadth of choice our ancestors would truly have envied. And today's armchair traveller can not only journey back in time, but also around the world in search of colour inspirations. To our Western history of colour associations can be added traditions from Mexico, India, Africa and the Far East. The pulsating electric combinations of Central and South America, the wonderful earthy palette of Africa, the subtle neutrals of Japan, the hot swirling pinks and reds of Rajasthan or the singing ice-cream colours of the Caribbean are becoming as familiar and accessible as Williamsburg blue or Gustavian grey. As the world around us shrinks, so our colour horizons broaden in response to new experiences.

From these cultural sources, we can really appreciate the excitement of intense colour. Unlike the subtle modulations of our traditional decorating palette, these saturated shades are used in sharp contrasts to brighten and enliven houses, inside and out. The contrasts may underscore architectural detail, as the deep blues used to pick out frames and architraves on Greek island houses, or simply set up vibrating oppositions. Painted shutters, doors, verandahs, balconies and window frames clash happily with walls in a joyous use of colour for its own sake. In parts of the world where resources are limited, luxuries few and far between, the sheer richness of colour delights the spirit.

COLOUR IN THE INTERIOR

STRONG COLOUR
GLIMPSED FROM A
HALLWAY CREATES A
SENSE OF SURPRISE
AND INVITATION.

Colour is not an abstraction. How we use it in our homes depends on a whole host of factors, including space, proportion, light and texture.

One persistent decorating convention says that small rooms, particularly small dark rooms, should be decorated in light colours to open them out and make them less confining. This argument is often used to justify decorating halls in neutral shades. I believe, on the contrary, that small rooms can take quite bright colours and that it is far better to accept their limitations and give them a jewel-like brilliance which compensates for the lack of space. In a situation where natural light levels are relatively low, strong colour intensifies and becomes richer, which is an added advantage. Warm colours – the reds, yellows and oranges – are 'advancing', and it is this characteristic that makes rooms painted in warm shades seem welcoming and intimate.

Halls, stairs and connecting areas are places people use frequently but for limited amounts of time, so bright colour here can be especially uplifting. The glimpse of an intensely coloured hall through an open doorway is inviting; a core of colour running from top to bottom draws the whole house together.

The other side of this approach is that in rooms which enjoy a great deal of natural light, light colours emphasize the airy spacious atmosphere. Pastels or subtly differentiated neutrals can be very reviving in these circumstances.

Another factor to consider when choosing colours is texture. Matt surfaces which absorb light – such as emulsion paint and unglazed cotton – look lighter in colour than shiny ones which reflect light – such as polished marble, satin and glazed chintz.

All colour schemes have to start somewhere – a favourite colour, or those in a treasured rug, a painting, a piece of pottery; this introduction may have provided some idea of where to look for inspiration. The following chapters focus on individual shades, their associations, folklore and special qualities; but each colour is a starting point for a multiplicity of combinations, which is where the excitement of exploring with colour really begins.

WHITE

'AND ALL WOKE EARLIER FOR THE UNACCUSTOMED BRIGHTNESS OF THE WINTER DAWNING, THE STRANGE HEAVENLY GLARE: THE EYE MARVELLED – MARVELLED AT THE DAZZLING WHITENESS . . .'

LONDON SNOW,

INTRODUCTION

White is a powerful, ancient colour. At once ordinary and dynamic, it is the traditional colour in the West for wedding dresses, a symbol of purity and chastity. The colour of ghosts and apparitions, white is worn as mourning in Asia, while in Africa white painted on the outside of dwellings wards off evil.

White interiors are cool and calm. At the same time white rooms are challenging to live in, uncompromising and revealing – an all-white scheme is not the easy option it might at first appear. In such pure surroundings the emphasis falls on texture; using white can be an exercise in exploring the richness of textural variety. Think of the soft translucence of white marble, the fine nap of freshly washed damask, the delicate filigree of lace or the crisp taut weave of canvas.

White is naturally a foil for other colours. (In fact, it can be misleading to call white a colour at all, since it represents white light in which all colours are blended.) Used with practically any other shade, white adds a look of freshness. Used with a selection of strong primaries, white can confer a Mondrian-

like modernity. White's classic partner is, of course, its opposite black. Just as white varies in tone, black can encompass deep midnight blue-black, rusty brown-black and charcoal – Van Gogh claimed to have identified 27 different shades of black in the paintings of Franz Hals. The monochromatic palette of many of the Dutch masters can be inspirational – lace collars over black velvet, black and white checked floors. Closer to our time, white and black suggest modernism, the grainy realism of the black and white photograph. Used in small quantities, as a detail, black has the effect of sharpening any colour scheme. A basic black and white combination can be very flexible, always offering the potential for dropping in other colours incidentally, with the use of flowers or decorative objects, a fluid approach which is well suited to city living. In the same way, using black and white in a kitchen will play on the technology of kitchen equipment and machinery, with the colours of fresh fruit and vegetables providing a contrast.

A HARMONY OF PURE WHITE MAKES A SERENE, CONTEMPLATIVE SPACE IN A HOUSE IN FRANCE.

WHITE LIGHT

WHITE ENLARGES A SPACE AND EMPHASIZES NATURAL LIGHT. IN THIS COOL COUNTRY INTERIOR THE PLAIN WHITE WALLS, TILED FLOOR AND THE DARK WOOD OF THE FURNITURE ARE COMPLEMENTED BY SNOW-WHITE CURTAINS AND THE SIMPLEST TABLECLOTH, ALL EDGED IN A NARROW FRINGED SEERSUCKER BRAID OF DARK BLUE AND WHITE CHECK. THE SIMPLICITY OF THIS WHITE FURNISHING IS GIVEN LIFT AND SPIRIT BY THE DEFINING LINE OF THE TRIMMING. WHEN COMBINING JUST TWO WHITES – HERE, ON WALLS AND IN FABRIC – THEY SHOULD BE BROADLY SIMILAR IN TONE, OTHERWISE THE WARMER VERSION WILL LOOK FAINTLY DISCOLOURED BY CONTRAST.

OLD WHITE

SOFT, 'DIRTY' WHITES – THE BEAUTIFUL MELLOW WHITES OF DISTEMPER, LIMEWASH AND WHITEWASH – AGE WELL AND SUIT THE FADED CHARACTER OF WELL-WORN WOOD AND OLD FABRIC. HERE, A LENGTH OF FILMY WHITE COTTON TIED ABOVE THE ARCHITRAVE MAKES A DELIGHTFUL FLOURISH FOR A WINDOW WHERE SCREENING THE LIGHT IS NOT A PRIORITY (ABOVE LEFT). BY PAINTING THE WOOD PANELLING AND

BEDHEAD WHITE, A COOL DELICATE LOOK WITH WARM MELLOW UNDERTONES CAN BE ACHIEVED (ABOVE RIGHT). SCANDINAVIA IS THE HOME OF LIGHT, AIRY PAINTED DECORATION. AND PALE SCRUBBED BOARDS AND DELICATE PAINTED FURNITURE ARE THE ESSENCE OF SCANDINAVIAN COUNTRY STYLE. TO CREATE THIS ATMOSPHERE, USE MATT EMULSION TO SIMULATE AN AGED PATINA (RIGHT).

CLASSICAL STRIPE

EVEN WITH A MUTED
PALETTE OF GREYS AND
WHITES, IT IS STILL POSSIBLE
TO ACHIEVE GREAT
LIVELINESS AND VARIETY.
THE STRENGTH OF THE
VARYING GEOMETRIC
PRINTS USED ON THESE
CHAIRS AND STOOLS IS
COUNTERBALANCED BY THE
CLASSICAL CHARCOAL-
AND-WHITE STRIPE FABRIC
WITH BUNCHES OF YELLOW
AURICULAS, AND THE IVY
PRINT USED TO COVER THE
TOP OF A FOOTSTOOL.
THERE ARE MANY DIFFERENT
SHADES OF WHITE AND ITS
NEAR-RELATIVE GREY:
EXPLOIT THESE SUBTLE
DIFFERENCES TO CREATE A
TIMELESS, CONTEMPLATIVE
AND RELAXING MOOD.

INTRODUCTION

Blue is an ascending colour. Like the lift in one's spirits when the sky is blue, or the feeling of infinity looking up at the heavens, blue is airy and expansive, generating a supreme sense of well-being. It reminds us of distance, space, sea and sky.

Perhaps because it is a colour which occurs widely in nature, blue is peaceful and refreshing, not tiring or overly exciting. Blue bedrooms are restful, blue bathrooms suitably watery. Blue was once considered to be the best colour for a kitchen because it was thought to keep flies away, although to our eyes, blue seems at home in the kitchen because of the long decorative tradition of blue and white china and tiles.

Blue is undoubtedly from the 'cool' side of the spectrum but it would be wrong to assume that this means it is invariably cold. The wrong shade of blue in the wrong conditions of light can be uncomfortable, which may well have led to blue's more negative associations with sorrow and gloom. Yet blues vary incredibly from almost violet to powder blue, from navy to the luminous singing blue of delphiniums and cornflowers.

Natural blue, from the organic vegetable dye indigo, was for many centuries the only affordable version of the colour. The precious mineral lapis lazuli gave an intense blue but was too expensive for use in the interior: rare and exclusive, it was the special blue of the Madonna's robes in early paintings, signifying her exalted status. Prussian blue, developed in the early eighteenth century, and synthetic blues in the nineteenth century, widened the blue palette.

Blue is valuable in decorating not merely for its fresh, vitalizing qualities, but also because it works so well with many other colours. Blue and white has a tradition of use all its own. Through sheer familiarity it has come to be the most domestic of colour combinations — the blue and white of countless kitchen plates, mattress ticking, checked gingham. A more electric pairing is the contrast of the opposites blue and yellow. Whether the combination is grand dark blue patterned with gold stars, or sky blue accented with lemon yellow, the effect is invigorating. And blues acquire depth in combination with greens and reds.

BUILT-IN SHELVES AND KITCHEN DRESSER IN A PRUSSIAN BLUE — A SURPRISING CHOICE FOR THIS BRETON HOUSE.

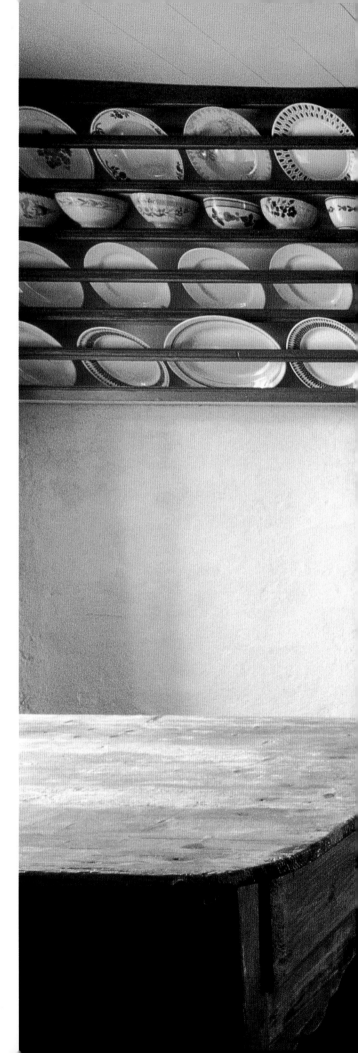

FRENCH BLUE

THE ELEGANCE OF NATURAL BLUE, LIKE INDIGO WHICH FADES TO A SOFT WARM COLOUR, IS DISPLAYED IN THIS FRENCH BEDROOM WITH ITS TIME-WORN BLUE-GREY PANELLING. THE CAST IRON BED HAS A COVERLET IN A BOLD, TEXTURED STRIPE, WHICH COMBINES EFFORTLESSLY WITH THE PAINTERLY CHECK FABRIC USED FOR PILLOWCASES AND CHAIR COVERING. AT THE TALL WINDOW, A DROP OF FABRIC VERTICALLY BANDED WITH A CLASSICALLY STYLIZED DESIGN, ADDS SOPHISTICATION TO THE COMPOSITION. THE THREE FABRICS WORK WELL BECAUSE, ASIDE FROM THEIR COMMON COLOURS, EACH HAS AN INHERENTLY GEOMETRIC STRUCTURE. WHEN PLACING DIFFERENT PATTERNS TOGETHER, THERE SHOULD ALWAYS BE SOME BASIC AFFINITY BETWEEN THE DESIGNS.

GUSTAVIAN GREY

THE FAMILY OF GREY-BLUES AND BLUE-GREYS IS STRONGLY ASSOCIATED WITH THE GUSTAVIAN PERIOD OF EIGHTEENTH-CENTURY SWEDEN. SCANDINAVIAN DECORATION OF ALL ERAS DEMONSTRATES A LOVE OF LIGHT, AND THE PARTICULAR ATTRACTION OF THESE COOL SHADES IS THAT THEY ENHANCE NATURAL LIGHT AND BRIGHTEN ROOMS.

A PAINTED BLUE CHAIR, BLUE CUPBOARD DOORS AND STRIPED BEDHANGINGS MAKE SIMPLE AND FRESH BEDROOM DECORATION (ABOVE). THE IDIOSYNCRATIC WALLPAINTING IN AN EIGHTEENTH-CENTURY SWEDISH INTERIOR IS SET OFF BY RICH BLUE-GREY DADOS AND DOORWAYS, EFFECTIVE BECAUSE OF THE SHEER REPETITION OF COLOUR (RIGHT).

CHECKS
AND
SPOTS

BLUE AND WHITE LOOK BEST
WHEN USED IN THE FORM
OF COOL GEOMETRIC
DESIGNS IN SPOTS, STRIPES
AND CHECKS, LIVELY
PATTERNS WHICH CAN BE
LAYERED IN HUNDREDS OF
DIFFERENT COMBINATIONS
– THE SIMPLEST AND MOST
FOOLPROOF FORM OF
PATTERN MIXING. THE
VARIETY OF MOODS AND
EFFECTS THAT CAN BE
ACHIEVED BY COMBINING
THESE TWO COLOURS IS
SEEMINGLY ENDLESS, FROM
PRETTY DELICATE SPOTTED
DESIGNS TO FORTHRIGHT
CHECKS, FRESH AND
UPLIFTING.

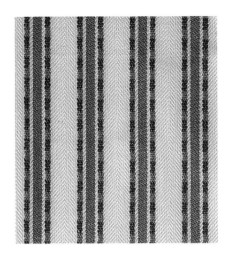  

  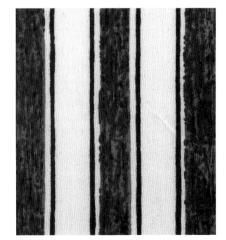

BLUE AND WHITE

A CLASSIC COMBINATION, BLUE AND WHITE IS
REFRESHING, CHARMING AND UTTERLY HARMONIOUS.
THE FASHION FOR BLUE-AND-WHITE DECORATION
PROBABLY DATES FROM THE SEVENTEENTH CENTURY
WHEN CHINESE PORCELAIN BEGAN ARRIVING IN
QUANTITIES IN THE WEST. TODAY THIS PARTNERSHIP
SUGGESTS EVERYDAY USE – ON TILES, CROCKERY AND
TICKING – MORE THAN EXOTIC DECORATION BUT IS NO
LESS POWERFUL OR APPEALING. DELFT TILES AND
PORTUGUESE *AZULEJOS* ARE TWO EXAMPLES OF
BLUE-AND-WHITE TILE TRADITIONS, WHILE PERHAPS THE
FINEST OF ALL CERAMIC ART DATES FROM
SIXTEENTH-CENTURY ISTANBUL WHERE BLUE-AND-
WHITE AND TURQUOISE TILES EMBELLISHED EVERY
SURFACE OF MOSQUES AND PALACES. IN FABRIC, THE
BLUE-AND-WHITE COMBINATION LENDS ITSELF TO
GEOMETRIC DESIGNS OF CHECKS.

LAVENDER BLUE

MAUVE, LAVENDER AND ICE BLUE ARE COOL, REFRESHING COLOURS, MUCH ENHANCED BY WHITE. AND IT IS IN THIS COMBINATION THAT THESE PARTICULAR SHADES OF BLUE ARE MOST OFTEN SEEN, DECORATING THE OUTSIDES OF HOUSES FROM NORTH AFRICA TO GREECE, REFLECTING LIGHT WITH A DAZZLING INTENSITY. LAVENDER, WITH ITS WARM UNDERTONES OF RED, IS THE LIGHTEST AND EASIEST OF THE COLOUR FAMILY BASED ON MIXTURES OF BLUE AND RED.

PURPLE CAN BE NOTORIOUSLY DIFFICULT TO HANDLE THOUGH. ONCE SO RARE AND PRECIOUS, ITS USE WAS EXCLUSIVELY RESERVED FOR ELEVATED ASSOCIATIONS. LAVENDER, ON THE OTHER HAND, IS AS FRESH AND COUNTRIFIED AS ITS NAME. SOOTHING, SHARP AND VITALIZING, IT LOOKS GOOD PLACED AGAINST ITS NATURAL PARTNER WHITE, OR USED WITH ACCENTS OF YELLOW AND GREEN.

ITALIAN CHECK

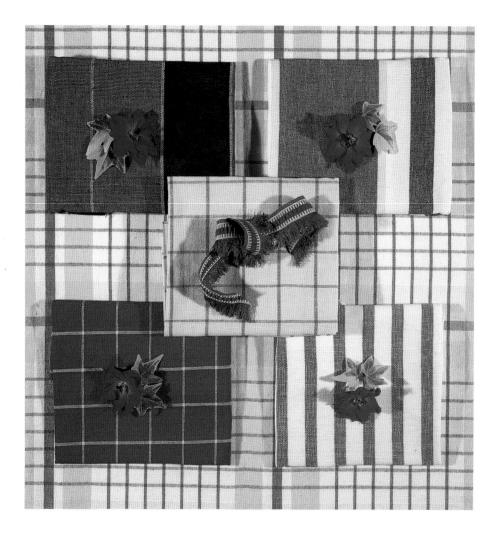

SOFT FURNISHING IN THE FORM OF LOOSE COVERING OR UPHOLSTERY CAN BE AN IMPORTANT MEANS OF INJECTING COLOUR IN TO AN ESSENTIALLY NEUTRAL ROOM, WHERE WALLS ARE WHITE AND FLOORS ARE NATURAL WOOD OR TILE. THE SINGING CONTRAST OF CLEAR YELLOW AND COBALT BLUE UNITES A GROUP OF CHECKED AND STRIPED FABRICS. THE VIBRANT COMBINATION OF BLUE AND YELLOW IS PARTICULARLY INVIGORATING IN STRONG LIGHT AND OFFERS A GREAT DEAL OF DECORATIVE POTENTIAL. THE COLOURS CAN BE SET OFF AGAINST EACH OTHER WHILE BALANCED WITHIN THE SAME GEOMETRIC PRINT, OR USED AS BLOCKS OF SOLID COLOUR, OR SEEN IN UNEQUAL PROPORTIONS WITH ONE COLOUR AS SHARP ACCENT TRIMMING FOR A MAIN FABRIC.

BLUE AND YELLOW

THIS IS AN ELECTRIC, NATURAL PARTNERSHIP: THE SUN
IN A SUMMER SKY; THE YELLOW CENTRE OF A BLUE
FLOWER; BRIGHT SUNLIGHT DAPPLED ON WATER.
PERSIAN MINIATURES EMBELLISHED WITH GOLD AND
LAPIS LAZULI; MEDIEVAL BOOKS OF HOURS WITH
GILDED LETTERING AND RICH, GLOWING BLUE
BACKGROUNDS SHOW THE DAZZLING RICHNESS OF
THE COMBINATION. AT THE SAME TIME, WHEN BLUE
AND YELLOW ARE MIXED TOGETHER, THEY PRODUCE
GREEN AND THE CENTRAL HARMONY AND BALANCE OF
THIS COLOUR IS IMPLICIT IN BLUE AND YELLOW
SCHEMES. ULTRAMARINE AND GOLD, SKY BLUE AND
SUNSHINE YELLOW, LIGHT BLUE AND PRIMROSE, WHEAT
GOLD AND DUCK-EGG, THE MOST SUCCESSFUL
PAIRINGS OF THE TWO COLOURS ARE THOSE WHICH
MATCH EACH OTHER TONALLY.

AQUAMARINE

THE INTRIGUING SHADE OF AQUAMARINE, THE
COLOUR OF THE WATER OVER THE SHELVING SEA
FLOOR, IS WHERE BLUE MEETS GREEN. BOLD AND
COMPELLING, YET RESTFUL AT THE SAME TIME, IT IS A
SHADE OFTEN FOUND IN COUNTRIES WHERE THE LIGHT
IS BRIGHT AND STRONG, SOMETIMES PAINTED ON THE
LOWER HALF OF THE WALL AS A DADO, WITH
WHITEWASH APPLIED OVER THE UPPER PORTION OF THE
WALL. NEITHER COOL NOR NEUTRAL, THIS BLUE IS A
CHALLENGING COLOUR FOR A LIVING ROOM OR
BEDROOM, STIMULATING BUT NOT TIRING ON THE EYE.
A BOLD VERSION OF THE COLOUR IS TYPICAL OF
TUNISIAN DECORATION; THE JOLTING COLOUR
CONTRASTS OF NORTH AFRICA HAVE PROVIDED
INSPIRATION FOR MANY TWENTIETH-CENTURY ARTISTS,
NOTABLY PAUL KLEE AND MATISSE.

BLUE AND GREEN

'BLUE AND GREEN SHOULD NEVER BE SEEN...' IS ONE FOLK
SAYING THAT MAKES VERY LITTLE SENSE. BLUE AND GREEN ARE
SEEN EVERYWHERE TOGETHER. WHERE SKY MEETS GREEN HILLS
OR SEASCAPE, THE SPECTRUM FROM VIOLET TO BLUE TO
AQUAMARINE TO GREEN BLENDS EFFORTLESSLY. THE EDGINESS
OF THE TWO COLOURS HAS LONG BEEN A SOURCE OF
FASCINATION, ESPECIALLY THE RANGE OF BLUE-GREENS, FROM
JADE TO TURQUOISE AND SEAGREEN. TURQUOISE, A
POWERFUL ANCIENT COLOUR MUCH PRIZED IN TIBET, ALSO
INTRIGUED THE EGYPTIANS, INCAS AND PERSIANS.
APOTHECARY BLUE, A PALE BLUE-GREEN, WAS A FAVOURITE
COLOUR OF FEDERAL AMERICA; A MUCH BRIGHTER VERSION
OF THE COLOUR IS SHOWN IN THE INTERIOR OF MOUNT
VERNON, GEORGE WASHINGTON'S HOME (CENTRE TOP).

GREEN

'IN MUSIC, ABSOLUTE GREEN IS REPRESENTED BY THE
PLACID, MIDDLE NOTES OF A VIOLIN.'

INTRODUCTION

Green represents balance and harmony. The product of total opposites blue and yellow, green is the colour of the landscape, the national colour of Ireland and the holy colour of Islam. In many cultures green is symbolic of the natural cycle of life and death – the Green Man and the Egyptian god of death, green-faced Osiris, both refer to this powerful connection. We mark the association more prosaically in the names we give different shades of green – leaf, olive, mint, grass, apple, lime. In counterpart to these associations are the negative connotations – green as the colour of envy and jealousy, or even betrayal, and the green of the serpent.

Green can also be elegant and sophisticated. The jade greens and celadons of the East, as well as neoclassical Adam greens, are extremely subtle colours, more suggestive of culture and refinement than the glories of nature. The Aesthetes at the end of the nineteenth century adopted a particular shade of yellow-green, promptly satirized by Gilbert and Sullivan as 'greenery-yallery', as a symbol of their precious artistic sensitivities.

Green is easy on the eye. At one time green was thought to be beneficial for the eyesight, and sunblinds made of green fabric were a common way of filtering strong light. Similarly, green was used as a traditionally contemplative background for a library or study. Aside from these specific applications, green has a long history of use in the interior, on panelling and woodwork as well as fabric and furnishings. While green is most peaceful and perhaps most versatile in soft muted shades, bright vibrant greens were an outstanding feature of Empire rooms, a fashion fostered by Napoleon.

Just as many greens are found together in nature, most shades of green harmonize effortlessly, from fir green to sea green, grey-green to emerald. Green and white are another natural pair, delicate and countrified. Green and red are complementaries which work together in many interesting ways. Forest green and tomato red possess a cheerful folk-art quality; lighter greens and light reds or rose are also highly compatible.

TIME-WORN GREEN PANELLING MAKES A MELLOW BACKGROUND FOR THIS SCANDINAVIAN FARMHOUSE.

PISTACHIO

A LIGHT, COOL RESTFUL GREEN IS A GOOD CHOICE FOR A BACKGROUND IN A
BEDROOM THAT RECEIVES MORNING SUN. REFRESHING AND VITAL, THIS
PARTICULAR SHADE OF GREEN IS RATHER SHARPER THAN THE FAMOUS CELADON
ASSOCIATED WITH THE PORCELAIN OF THE SUNG DYNASTY, BUT IS EQUALLY
VERSATILE. THE CEILING AND FLOOR ARE LIGHT-TONED TO MAINTAIN THE AIRY
QUALITY OF THE ROOM. BLACK-AND-WHITE CHECKED UPHOLSTERY ON THE BED
AND STOOL GIVES A GRAPHIC BASE TO THE LIME, SAFFRON AND PURPLE CONTRASTS
OF THE FABRIC USED TO COVER THE BED.

FOREST GREEN

A ROOM DECORATED ALL IN SHADES OF GREEN COULD NEVER BE DULL OR DISCORDANT – THE GREENS OF NATURE VARY FROM THE DEEP FIR GREEN OF SPRUCE TREES TO THE BRIGHT YELLOW-GREEN OF NEW SPRING GROWTH, FROM SILVERY GREY ROSEMARY TO EMERALD TURF. CITRUS YELLOW AND FIR GREEN ARE A TRADITIONAL INTERIOR COMBINATION THAT BOASTS RATHER NORDIC ASSOCIATIONS, ESPECIALLY WHEN DISPLAYED IN THE FORM OF A BOLD CHECK PRINT (LEFT).

GARDEN

IN THE GARDEN, GREEN IS THE ANCHORING COLOUR, THE FOIL FOR EYE-CATCHING
SHADES OF FLOWERS AND FRUIT. IN THIS FARMHOUSE BEDROOM WITH ITS RAFTERED
CEILING, ALL THE SOFT TONALITIES OF THE FLOWER GARDEN ARE DISPLAYED IN THE
COMBINATION OF WILLOW, FIR AND LIME GREENS, SET AGAINST WARMER ROSE
AND GOLDEN YELLOWS. THE OVERSCALE FRUIT PATTERN ON THE FACING CURTAINS
HAS A WATERCOLOUR TRANSPARENCY WHICH SOFTENS THE BOLDNESS OF THE
DESIGN. BLUE-AND-WHITE UNDERCURTAINS ECHO THE GEOMETRIC UPHOLSTERY
OF THE CHAIR. HAVING TWO SETS OF CURTAINS AT THE WINDOW ENABLES ONE
LIGHT-FILTERING SET TO BE DRAWN WHEN THE SUN IS STRONG, WITH A FACING
OUTER CURTAIN RESERVED FOR SHEER DECORATIVE INTEREST.

SEASHORE

VIBRATING SHADES OF SEA GREEN AND LUMINOUS BLUE ARE FOUND ON THE SEASHORES OF THE MEDITERRANEAN AND CARIBBEAN, THE CHEERFUL OPPOSITION OF COLOUR PARTICULARLY BRILLIANT IN THE CLARITY OF THE LIGHT. GREEK-ISLAND HOUSES ARE OFTEN WHITEWASHED, OR COLOURWASHED IN FADED OCHRES, WITH DETAILS – DOORS, WINDOW FRAMES AND SHUTTERS – PAINTED IN SOFT, BRIGHT GREENS, BLUES AND GREYS. WATER-BASED VERSIONS OF THIS MEDITERRANEAN PALETTE ARE AVAILABLE AND EASY TO USE; COLOURS CAN BE READILY THINNED TO THE REQUIRED DEGREE OF INTENSITY (LEFT). CARIBBEAN COLOUR SENSE, DISPLAYED IN THE PAINTING OF THIS HAITIAN BEACHHOUSE, IS EXUBERANT AND FULL OF GAIETY, ITS BRIGHT CHALKY COLOURS GLEAM IN THE SUNSHINE (RIGHT).

APPLE
GREEN

A RUSTIC LOOK FOR A
DINING ROOM TEAMS A
WALLPAPER AND BORDER AT
DADO LEVEL WITH
CURTAINS IN A LARGE-
SCALE GARLAND PRINT. THE
SATURATED COLOURS OF
SHARP GREEN AND
GOLDEN YELLOW,
MEDIATED BY RUSSET, MAKE
A MELLOW BACKGROUND
FOR AN EATING ROOM,
WHERE THE ATMOSPHERE
CAN BE SOMEWHAT
THEATRICAL AND THE
QUALITY OF LIGHT ADDS TO
THE ENJOYMENT OF FOOD
AND CONVERSATION. A
STRICT COORDINATION OF
PAPER AND FABRIC CAN BE
DEADENING, WHEREAS THE
SUBTLE VARIATIONS IN
THESE DESIGNS,
REFLECTING THEIR
DIFFERENT APPLICATIONS,
IS MORE INTERESTING.

CHUTNEY

THE SPICY COMBINATION OF LIME AND MANGO
INSPIRES A LIVELY MIXTURE OF PATTERN IN A BEDROOM.
BEDS OFFER GREAT POTENTIAL FOR CONTRIBUTING
COLOUR AND PATTERN INTEREST: BED COVERS,
THROWS, QUILTS AND BLANKETS CAN DISPLAY A
SYMPHONY OF TONING AND CONTRASTING SHADES
FAR FROM THE BLAND AND NEUTRAL APPEARANCE OF
PLAIN BEDSPREADS OR QUILT COVERS. FURTHER
DRESSING IN THE FORM OF BOLSTER COVERS,
PILLOWCASES AND CUSHION COVERS REINFORCE THE
FURNISHED LOOK, MAKING THE BEDROOM A PLACE TO
RELAX IN AT ALL TIMES OF THE DAY.

GREEN 91

AUTHENTIC GREEN

GREEN IN ALL OF ITS VARIATIONS HAS BEEN ONE OF THE MOST PREVALENT COLOURS IN THE HISTORY OF DECORATION, EACH SHADE ASSOCIATED WITH A CHARACTERISTIC PERIOD OR STYLE. DEEP FIR-GREEN WAS A COMMON COLOUR FOR GEORGIAN PANELLING; BRIGHTER PEA-GREEN DATES FROM LATER IN THE EIGHTEENTH CENTURY. ROBERT ADAM MADE USE OF A VARIETY OF LIGHT GREENS AND BLUE-GREENS, WITH DIFFERENT SHADES DEFINING CHANGES IN MODELLING AND MOULDING. YELLOW-GREEN WAS AN IMPORTANT FEDERAL COLOUR, WHILE BRILLIANT GREEN WAS FAVOURED BY NAPOLEON AND WIDELY SEEN IN EMPIRE ROOMS. THE VICTORIANS ENJOYED MORE SOMBRE GREENS AND OLIVE SHADES, WITH A DULL VEGETABLE GREEN BEING PARTICULARLY ASSOCIATED WITH THE LATE NINETEENTH-CENTURY ARTS AND CRAFTS MOVEMENT. ALL SHADES OF TRADITIONAL GREEN LEND AN AIR OF REST AND RELAXATION TO BOTH LIVING ROOMS AND BEDROOMS.

YELLOW

'THE MAGIC OF THE SUN TRANSMUTES THE PALM TREES
INTO GOLD, THE WATER SEEMS FULL OF DIAMONDS AND
MEN BECOME KINGS FROM THE EAST.'

PIERRE AUGUSTE RENOIR,
WRITING OF ALGERIA

INTRODUCTION

Yellow is warm and enriching. The colour of sunlight, buttercups, lemons and gold, it draws the eye. It is inescapably cheerful, a bright uplifting colour that always strikes a positive note without becoming too insistent.

Like other colours, it has its special meanings. The saffron of monks' robes is a holy colour in Buddhism; while yellow's natural associations with the power of the sun and ripening grain make it a necessary part of harvest celebrations. Yellow (and its near-relative orange) are most notable for being particularly eye-catching, which goes some way to explaining their widespread use in packaging, graphics and signs – any application where being noticed quickly is of the utmost importance.

In decoration yellow – in its pure, clear form – was unknown before the manufacture of chrome yellow at the beginning of the nineteenth century, although quite surprisingly bright yellows using the earth pigment ochre were achieved before this time. The arrival of chrome yellow coincided with the neoclassical taste for brilliant colour; bright yellow was an Empire colour.

One of the best known yellow rooms of all is Monet's dining room at Giverny in France. The singing yellow walls give the effect of drenching the room with sunlight and make a vivid background for Monet's collection of Japanese prints. The clever combination of subtle and strong yellow shades at Giverny has provided inspiration for countless decorators. Equally influential in its dramatic use of yellow was the London drawing room of Nancy Lancaster, decorated in the 1950s in a warm rich shade of yellow which the American decorator nicknamed 'buttah yellah'. The strength and appeal of this colour scheme set a whole new fashion in English country-house style.

Yellow lightens and brightens any room. Traditionally a kitchen colour, where its natural vivacity promotes a cosy feeling of hospitality, it can also be a good choice for a bedroom, particularly one that benefits from early morning sun. On the other hand, a room that looks out on a dull grey city street might benefit enormously from a yellow-based scheme to counteract the lack of light. Light primrose yellows work well with greys and whites. The deeper versions of the colour stand up better in stronger combinations. Pure lemon yellow is a natural accompaniment to blues; the warmer mellow yellows can be beautifully complemented with crimsons and roses.

MONET'S FAMOUS DINING ROOM AT GIVERNY COMBINES PURE SUNSHINE
YELLOW WITH FORGET-ME-NOT BLUE TO OUTSTANDING EFFECT.

CHROME YELLOW

REALLY BRIGHT YELLOW WAS FIRST MANUFACTURED IN THE EARLY DECADES OF THE NINETEENTH CENTURY AND RAPIDLY GAINED FAVOUR. IN THE INTERIORS OF NEOCLASSICAL ARCHITECTS SUCH AS SIR JOHN SOANE, IT WAS COMBINED WITH BLACK AND WARM RED, AND THIS CONTEMPORARY SCHEME MAKES USE OF THE SAME DYNAMIC COMBINATION TO GREAT EFFECT. THE SELF-STRIPE OF THE FABRIC ON SOFA AND SCREEN HAS A GENTLY MODULATING EFFECT ON THE BLOCKS OF SOLID COLOUR, WITH THE SMALL TERRACOTTA FRINGE ADDING A SUITABLY COMPLEMENTARY TOUCH. THE PAIRING OF YELLOW AND BLACK HAS AN ESPECIALLY MODERN GRAPHIC QUALITY. BRIGHT COLOUR CAN BE A GOOD CHOICE FOR A HALLWAY, ENLIVENING AN OTHER-WISE 'LOST' AND CHARACTERLESS SPACE AND RUNNING LIKE A VIVID THREAD FROM LEVEL TO LEVEL, CONNECTING ROOMS AND VIEWS.

OCHRE

EARTH YELLOWS, DERIVED FROM OCHRE AND RAW SIENNA, HAVE A LONG HISTORY OF USE AROUND THE WORLD. ALTHOUGH THEY CAN BE SURPRISINGLY BRIGHT, LIKE OTHER EARTH COLOURS THEY NEVER ACHIEVE THE LUMINOSITY OF A TRUE PRIMARY. LIVELY AND WARM, EARTH YELLOWS MAKE EXCELLENT WALL COLOURS, SOFTENING THE LIGHT AND PROVIDING A GLOWING BACKGROUND FOR OTHER FURNISHING COLOURS. DERIVED LITERALLY FROM EARTH – FROM CLAY AND SAND – THESE PIGMENTS HAVE ALWAYS BEEN EASY TO FIND, HENCE THEIR WIDESPREAD USE, FROM AFRICA TO NORTHERN EUROPE. IN THIS GUJARAT MUD HUT ARE DELIGHTFUL SAFFRON-COVERED BEDS (ABOVE) AND NATURALLY WORN OCHRE-WASHED WALLS (RIGHT).

GOLD

THE QUALITY OF LIGHT CAN MAKE AN IMPORTANT DIFFERENCE TO THE WAY IN WHICH YELLOW IS PERCEIVED. LATE AFTERNOON LIGHT WITH ITS WARM GOLD TONES LENDS A SPECIAL RICHNESS TO THE MIXTURE OF BRIGHT YELLOW, GREEN AND TOUCHES OF RED AND BLUE. SOPHISTICATED AND LIGHT-ENHANCING, YELLOW IS OFTEN BEST DISPLAYED IN LARGER ROOMS, SUCH AS THIS DRAWING ROOM WITH ITS MELLOW PANELLING AND TALL WINDOW. THE SWATHE OF FABRIC PATTERNED WITH GARLANDS OF FRUIT BLENDS COMFORTABLY WITH THE SELF-STRIPED YELLOW OF THE LOOSE COVERING ON THE CHAIR. THE MEREST HINT OF RED AND BLUE ALONGSIDE YELLOW IN THE OTHER STRIPED FABRIC ON THE SOFA GIVES DEPTH AND BALANCE TO THE PRINT.

FEDERAL YELLOW

LIGHT PRIMROSE-YELLOW, AS WELL AS A STRONGER YELLOW-GREEN, WERE MUCH USED IN THE INTERIORS OF COLONIAL AND FEDERAL AMERICA. COLOUR IS AN IMPORTANT MEANS OF EXPRESSING AND ENHANCING RICH ARCHITECTURAL DETAIL, AS THE VIEW OF A SPLENDID EIGHTEENTH-CENTURY HALL IN HOMEWOOD HOUSE, BALTIMORE DISPLAYS. THE WHITE-COVED CEILING AND CRISP MOULDINGS ARE THROWN INTO RELIEF BY THE FRESH YELLOW WALLS AND PALE DUCK-EGG BLUE DETAIL (RIGHT). PRIMROSE AND MINT-STRIPED CURTAINS UNDER A FACING CURTAIN IN A FLOWERED STRIPE ADD FLAIR TO A SEATING AREA (LEFT).

YELLOW AND BLUE

YELLOW AND BLUE IS AN UPLIFTING COMBINATION. THE COLOURS OF SUNNY SUMMER DAYS, YELLOW WARMS AND BRIGHTENS, WHILE BLUE IS EXPANSIVE AND AIRY, MAKING A VERSATILE, STABLE PARTNERSHIP FOR ANY INTERIOR. THIS COLOUR COMBINATION CAN ALSO BE SUCCESSFUL OUTDOORS. A RUSH-SEATED CHAIR PAINTED BLUE SINGS OUT AGAINST WALLPAPER PATTERNED WITH MELLOW FRUIT, FULL OF SUN, A WARM COMBINATION OF COLOURS TYPICAL OF PROVENCE (RIGHT). SIMPLER, BUT NO LESS EFFECTIVE, IS THE ELECTRIC OPPOSITION OF THE TWO COLOURS IN THE PAINTED WALL AND BALCONY (ABOVE).

CITRUS

SHARP YELLOWS AND GREENS – THE CITRUS COLOURS
OF LEMON AND LIME – HAVE ALL THE FRESHNESS OF
EARLY SUMMER. MEDIATED BY WHITE THEY FORM A
VERSATILE COMBINATION IDEAL FOR BRIGHT ROOMS
WHICH RECEIVE A GOOD DEAL OF NATURAL LIGHT,
CRISP AND TAILORED IN STRIPES, LEMON, LIME AND
WHITE HAVE A MORE TRADITIONAL ASSOCIATION IN
RAVISHING CHINTZES. MAINTAIN THE HARMONY BY
COMBINING SHADES WHICH ARE EQUAL IN TONAL
STRENGTH. MIX BRIGHT WITH BRIGHT AND
JUXTAPOSE PALE WITH PALE FOR A GOOD EFFECT.

TUSCAN GLOW

THE SATURATED TONES OF ITALIAN LIGHT, FAMOUSLY WARM AND GOLDEN, ARE ECHOED IN THE CHOICE OF COLOURS IN THIS *AL FRESCO* SEATING AREA. THE BLEND OF YELLOW AND PINK ON THE DAY BED RELATE TO THE WARM PLASTER-PINK OF THE WALL, WHILE A LIGHT GREEN SERVES AS THE ACCENT, A FESTIVE MIXTURE OF SUMMER COLOURS. FOR THE ECONOMICALLY MINDED, CUSHIONS ARE A GOOD WAY OF RINGING THE CHANGES IN DECORATION, INTRODUCING A VARIETY OF PATTERNS AND COLOURS THAT ARE SUITABLE FOR EACH SEASON IN THE YEAR.

 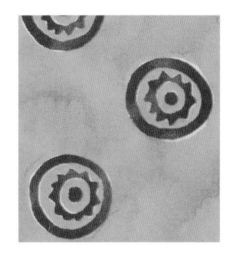 

YELLOW 115

YELLOW AND PINK

ONE MIGHT BE FORGIVEN FOR THINKING THAT SUCH STARTLING COMBINATIONS AS BRILLIANT-YELLOW AND MAGENTA COULD ONLY BE A PRODUCT OF THE MODERN SYNTHETIC WORLD. IT MAY BE SURPRISING, THEN, TO FIND THAT NATURE PROVIDES COLOUR SHOCKS THAT ARE EVERY BIT AS THRILLING AND SPECTACULAR AS THOSE CONCOCTED BY A COMMERCIAL PAINT MANUFACTURER. YELLOW AND PINK, AS SEEN IN THE BALINESE DISPLAY OF BOTTLES (LEFT), OR THE CLOSE-UP OF A GERBERA'S CENTRE (RIGHT) HAVE AMAZING VITALITY TOGETHER. TO MAKE THIS COLOUR COMBINATION WORK IN THE INTERIOR, MEDIATE THE SCHEME WITH A SHARP LIGHT GREEN.

NATURAL

'THE COLOURIST IS HE WHO SEEING A COLOUR IN
NATURE KNOWS AT ONCE HOW TO ANALYSE IT, AND
CAN SAY FOR INSTANCE: THAT GREEN-GREY IS YELLOW

INTRODUCTION

Nature abounds with colour, but the true natural palette encompasses a wonderfully subtle range of creams, grey-browns and biscuit shades, the colours of wood, stone and earth. Our enthusiasm for these warm neutrals has much to do with today's increasing appreciation of natural materials and ethnic craftwork. The traditional Japanese house, with its golden tatami mats and ricepaper screens, has been an important influence in this quest for natural simplicity.

Natural colours have long been the mainstay of home decoration. Buffs and browns are among the most widely used and accessible of all colours, readily available from earth pigments such as ochres and umbers. The appropriately termed 'drab' was a standard interior colour of the eighteenth and nineteenth century. Greys and creams reminiscent of weathered stone were also popular in Georgian houses. Brown was the colour for woodwork — doors, dados and panelling were painted naturalistically in 'wood' colours, an odd notion today when 'wood' colours are more likely to come from the natural material.

Natural colour schemes have an inherent simplicity. Rush matting or coir on the floor, earthenware pots, unbleached calicos and muslins, nubbly raw linens and silks, wickerwork and waxed wood have a pleasing textural variety that adds interest to the muted colour range. Yet natural colours can also be highly sophisticated. Using a range of narrowly differentiated shades to pick out architectural detailing – cornicing or plasterwork modelling, for example – was an approach much favoured by John Fowler in his colour schemes for grand historic houses.

Natural colours often work best on their own without the introduction of brighter, more saturated shades. But there is sufficient range and depth within the family of neutrals for this hardly to be a restriction; texture extends the scope still further. Walls painted in warm natural or muddied colours can be set off crisply by pure white ceilings and woodwork; black detailing can also give a sharp graphic edge. The best strong colours to accompany a natural scheme have some earthy quality to them as well – brick or Indian reds and warm indigo blues will not overwhelm the essential softness.

There are few rooms which will not suit this type of colour scheme. Natural rooms are restful, if rather retiring; there is an added freshness and simplicity which can be very appealing in bedrooms, living rooms and kitchens alike. A positive advantage is the opportunity to explore different materials, from quarry tiles and limed oak, to sisal and slate, and to enjoy the intrinsic beauty of these naturally occurring materials.

THE SOFT NATURAL TONES FROM CREAM TO BUFF, SUBTLE AND COMFORTABLE, HAVE BEEN USED IN DECORATION FOR CENTURIES.

DRIFTWOOD

THE SANDY COLOURS OF
NORTHERN SEASIDES,
BLEACHED BY SUN AND SEA,
COMPRISE A NATURALLY
HARMONIOUS FAMILY. THE
COUNTRIFIED SIMPLICITY
OF WHITE WALLS AND TILED
FLOOR HAS BEEN CARRIED
OVER INTO THE STYLE OF
FURNISHING, WITH A
SAND-AND-BLACK
CHECKED PATTERN USED TO
COVER A CHAIR AND A
SIMILAR RUST-AND-BISCUIT
CHECKED FABRIC
CURTAINING A DOORWAY,
BENEATH A FACING
DRAPERY OF MUTED STONE
COLOURS. IMPORTANT
ELEMENTS ARE THE BLACK
DETAILS IN THE CHAIR
UPHOLSTERY AND CURTAIN
FRINGING, WHICH ADD
STRENGTH TO THE SOFT
TONAL RANGE. CURTAINS
FOR DOORWAYS – ONCE
CALLED PORTIERES – MAKE
SENSE IN WARM AND COOL
CLIMATES ALIKE. IN
NORTHERN COUNTRIES,
THEY PROVIDE EXCELLENT
INSULATION AGAINST
DRAUGHTS; IN WARM
AREAS OF THE WORLD, THEY
SCREEN STRONG LIGHT
AND HELP KEEP INTERIORS
COOL IN THE DAYTIME.

NATURAL   127

NATURE STUDY

BROWN IS TOO PLAIN A TERM FOR THE RICH TONES OF
WOOD, STONE AND EARTH WHICH COMPRISE THE
NATURAL PALETTE. A STRIP OF BARK, A PIECE OF
DRIFTWOOD, CORN COBS, WEATHERED CARVING, OLD
STONE WALLS – YOU CAN LOOK AT ANY ONE OF A
NUMBER OF NATURAL MATERIALS AND SEE A WEALTH OF
DISTINCT SHADES AND NUANCES OF TONE FROM
CHARCOAL TO BUFF, TOBACCO-BROWN TO BISCUIT.
ALL OF THESE SHADES HAVE A LONG HISTORY OF USE IN
THE INTERIOR. BROWNS OF VARIOUS HUES WERE THE
TRADITIONAL COLOURS FOR DOORS AND
WOODWORK; LIGHTER BUFFS AND 'DRAB' NATURAL
SHADES WERE COMMON WALL COLOURS FOR SEVERAL
CENTURIES. SET AGAINST SPARKLING WHITE DETAIL
AND A HINT OF BLACK FOR DEPTH, THEY HAVE THE
POWER TO CREATE ROOMS OF EXCEPTIONAL
REFINEMENT AND RESTFULNESS.

FRESCO

THE WARM BUFF COLOUR OF NATURAL PLASTER IS THE IDEAL BACKGROUND FOR
A DINING ROOM. THE COLOUR LOOKS SOFT AND TRANQUIL WITH DAYLIGHT
STREAMING THROUGH FRENCH WINDOWS; AT NIGHT, UNDER CANDLELIGHT, IT
COMES ALIVE, WITH THE GLOWING COLOURS OF FOOD SINGING OUT IN
CONTRAST. SUCH NEUTRAL TONES, NEITHER ENCLOSING NOR RETREATING,
CREATE AN ATMOSPHERE OF SPACE AND LIGHT IDEAL FOR AN EATING ROOM.
PLAIN PLASTER CAN BE TOO PINK IN ITS UNTREATED STATE, AND MUST BE SEALED
IN ANY CASE BECAUSE DUST FORMS ON ITS SURFACE. A TONING WASH OR
GLAZE GIVES DEPTH WITHOUT LOSING THE NATURAL COLOUR.

TERRACOTTA

'GIVE ME MUD AND I WILL PAINT THE SKIN OF VENUS.'

INTRODUCTION

This family of earth colours complements the natural palette of neutral shades. Terracotta, literally 'fired earth', includes a range of warm rich colours from pale plaster-pinkish red to deep earth-red, with hot oranges somewhere in between. The basis for many of these colours are earth pigments, particularly those which are heated or roasted – burnt sienna and burnt umber, for example – to give deeper, more fiery shades.

These old colours, found inside and outside houses in practically every culture around the world, can be quite bright, although they lack the pure brilliance of primaries. Their softness and warmth make them easy to live with; the glow reflected from warm terracotta walls is exceptionally flattering, while the light in such rooms at all times of the day is beautifully golden, reminiscent of Mediterranean evenings.

Terracotta is emphatically not 'peach'. Peach, especially in its recent, more fashionable manifestations, can be remarkably insipid, the result of omitting the essential element of earthiness. Real terracotta suggests raw plaster, sun-dried earth, and warm sandstone.

Because of these associations it can often be effective to exaggerate the textural dimension. Paint can be applied in a bold wash or stippled to show patches of unevenness redolent of a rough-baked surface. This rather rustic effect is very compatible with the mellow tones of old polished wood.

Darker versions, tending towards a deep red-brown, work well with the refreshing contrast of blue or black and white. Blue and white crockery, black and white tiled floors, and checked or striped fabric all go well with a deep terracotta background. The look is not invariably countrified; the warm tones of any of these colours give an extra dimension of warmth and light in the city.

The clearest and least earthy of all the terracotta colours is orange, a colour that is particularly associated with the wonderful checked fabrics of Madras. Orange, historically, was one of the fashionable shades of Art Deco, teamed with sharp lime green and cool blue. Orange and cool green make a fresh, invigorating combination.

THE WARMTH OF TERRACOTTA ON ROOF TILES AND WALLS ENRICHES THIS MEXICAN TERRACE.

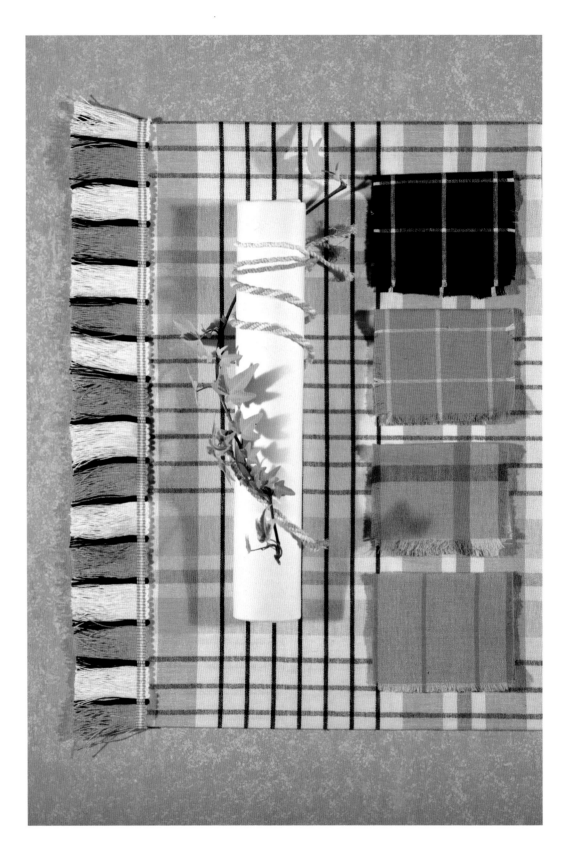

CORAL

THIS WARMING SUN-DRENCHED COLOUR SCHEME FOR A BEDROOM IS BASED AROUND A PARTICULAR BURNT-ORANGE SHADE, SLIGHTLY BRIGHTER THAN TRUE TERRACOTTA, MORE EARTHY THAN ORANGE. A BLIND IN A DAPPLED PATTERN TINTS THE LIGHT WHILE BED CURTAINS IN A WARM CHECK ADD TO THE MELLOW, GLOWING ATMOSPHERE. ANY ROOM WHICH FACES NORTH OR LACKS NATURAL LIGHT WOULD BENEFIT FROM SUCH ENRICHING COLOURS. EVEN IF BED CURTAINS ARE NO LONGER A PRACTICAL NECESSITY IN CENTRALLY HEATED HOMES, THEY RETAIN THEIR DECORATIVE IMPACT, COUNTERBALANCING THE EXPANSE OF THE BED AND OFFERING THE OPPORTUNITY FOR INJECTING LIVELY AREAS OF COLOUR AND PATTERN INTO A ROOM.

BRICK AND BLACK

TERRACOTTA COLOURS
PRODUCE THE MOST
FLATTERING BACKGROUND,
EITHER PAINTED ON THE
WALLS TO REFLECT LIGHT,
OR HUNG AT THE
WINDOWS, FOR LIGHT TO
FILTER SOFTLY THROUGH.
THESE WARM-TO-HOT
COLOURS WORK WELL WITH
COLOURS OF A SIMILAR
STRENGTH AND INTENSITY –
A VIVID STREAK OF LIME,
FOR EXAMPLE AND, OF
COURSE, BLACK. AT THE
WINDOW, HOT, DEEP
TERRACOTTA AND BUFF-
STRIPED UNDERCURTAINS
HAVE FACING CURTAINS IN
A BOLD FRUIT PRINT. THE
CHAIRS ARE IN RICH
CONTRASTING PRINTS:
BLACK AND LIME SELF-
STRIPE ALL COMPLEMENTED
BY A CLASSIC BLACK-AND-
WHITE MARBLE FLOOR.

SPICE

'SPICE' COLOURS FORM AN IMPORTANT PART OF THE TERRACOTTA COLOUR SPECTRUM. HERE, A PANELLED ROOM IS THE SETTING FOR A MIXTURE OF BRIGHT YELLOW, DEEP RED, AND SAFFRON AND NUTMEG-BROWN, ALL DISPLAYED ON THE UPHOLSTERY OF SOFAS AND A COVERED STOOL. A ROOM MAY HAVE NEUTRAL-TONED WALLS AND FLOOR AND LITTLE IN THE WAY OF WINDOW TREATMENT YET STILL RETAIN A STRONG COLOUR CHARACTER. THIS CAN BE ACHIEVED THROUGH THE JUDICIOUS USE OF SOFT FURNISHING, IN THE FORM OF UPHOLSTERY OR LOOSE COVERING.

AUTUMN

THE TERRACOTTA PALETTE ENCOMPASSES THE AUTUMN
RANGE OF COLOURS, FROM SHARP ORANGE TO RUSSET
AND AUBERGINE, THE STRONG EARTH COLOURS
DISPLAYED ON MEDIEVAL ENCAUSTIC FLOORS, RIPE
FRUIT AND HARVEST VEGETABLES SUCH AS MARROWS
AND PUMPKINS, A BEECH WOOD WHEN THE LEAVES
HAVE TURNED, THE CORALS AND BLUSH ORANGES OF
SEASHELLS ARE STRIKING COLOUR INSPIRATIONS. IN
THE INTERIOR, TERRACOTTA NATURALLY COMES IN THE
FORM OF TILED FLOORS AND WARM WOOD TONES;
LIGHTER VERSIONS OF THE COLOUR IN THE APPEALING
COLOUR OF RAW PLASTER, CHARMINGLY UNEVEN AND
WARM IN TONE, SUCH COLOURS ARE VERY CLOSE TO
THE POMPEIIAN RED WHICH SO ENTRANCED THE
ARCHITECTS AND DESIGNERS OF THE
NINETEENTH-CENTURY NEOCLASSICAL PERIOD.

MADRAS

AN EASY WAY TO DRESS A BED IS TO THROW A LENGTH OF CLOTH OVER A SIMPLE ARMATURE
AND ALLOW IT TO DRAPE TO EITHER SIDE. THE DEEP SHELL-PINK AND TERRACOTTA COLOURS
OF THIS COMBINATION RECALL THE WONDERFUL MIXTURES IN TRADITIONAL MADRAS
PATTERNS: CLEAR ORANGE, PINK, YELLOW AND GREEN IN SUBTLE CHECKS AND STRIPES. THE
KELIM CARPET DISPLAYS ALL THE COLOURS IN THE ROOM. A FAVOURITE RUG, PAINTING OR
PIECE OF POTTERY CAN BE A FRUITFUL STARTING POINT FOR DECORATIVE IDEAS.

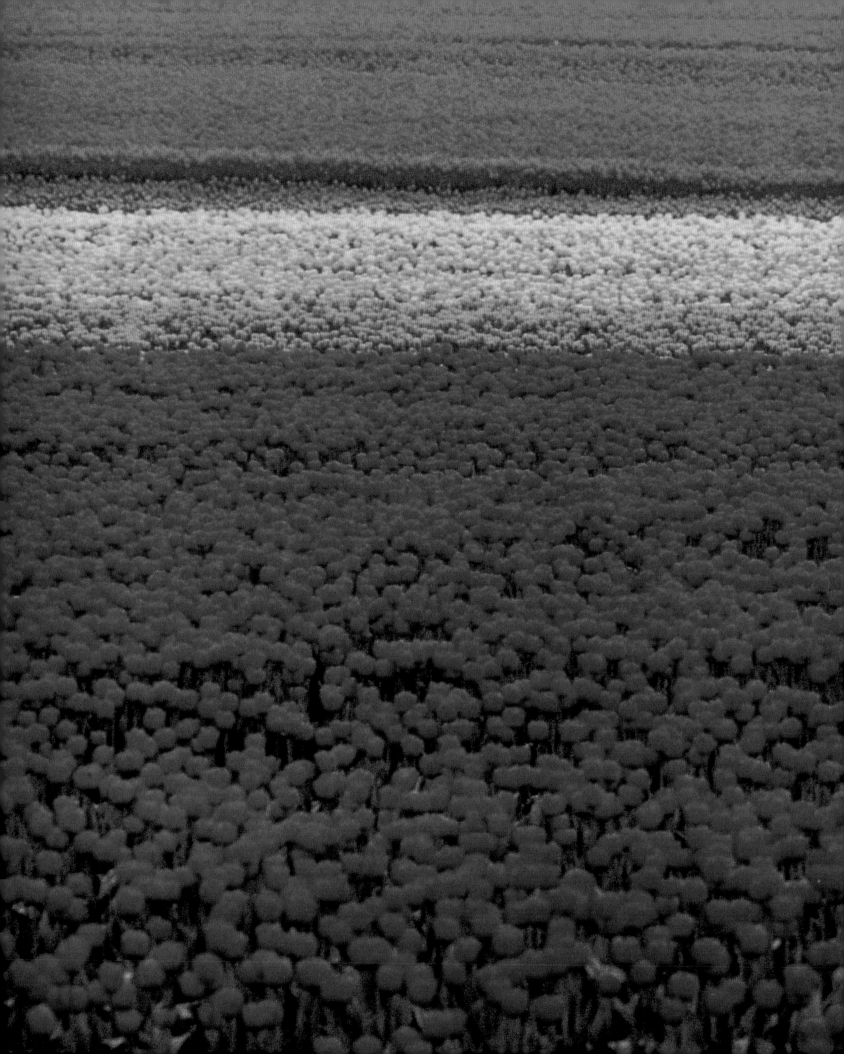

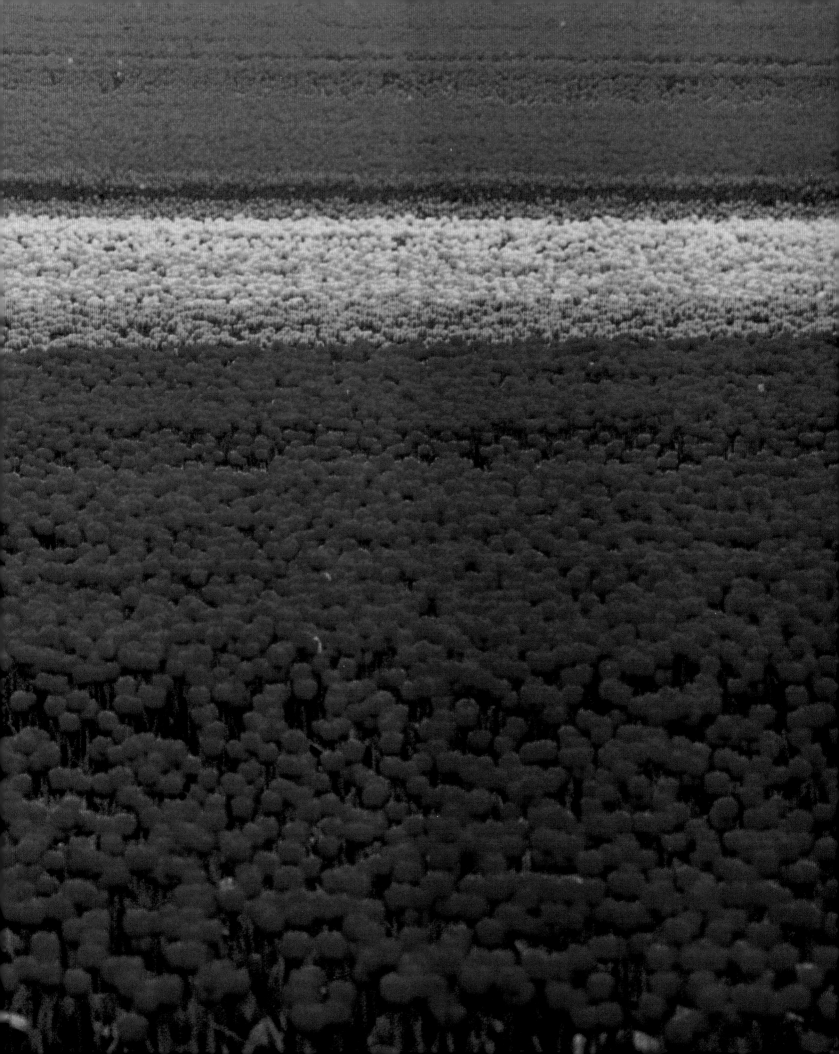

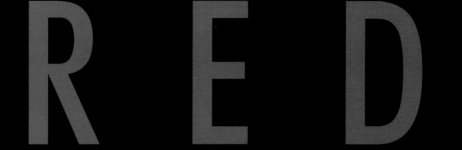

RED

'A FIERCE VINDICTIVE SCRIBBLE OF RED.'

INTRODUCTION

Red arouses. Hot, passionate, rich and celebratory, red is a siren shade, a colour to revel in. The Chinese colour of luck and happiness, the marriage colour of India, red is the colour of love and romance, of courage, passion and rage. Red means danger, stop, fire; in nature, red is the accent that signals the poisonous berries, the ripe fruit or the bright courtship display. It is uniquely assertive and vigorous.

In decoration red has always signified richness and luxury. This basic association is hardly surprising since pigments and dyes giving bright vivid reds were expensive and rare until the new synthetic colours of the mid-nineteenth century were introduced. Early on in the history of interior design, red silk damask stretched over the walls was the height of sophisticated display and made a sumptuous glowing background in glittering state rooms. Red was believed to be the best foil for paintings; as well as in galleries, red walls often featured in dining rooms or grand rooms otherwise used for entertaining, where the intention was to generate excitement and show off wealth.

Today many people are wary of using red in large quantities, just as they hesitate before using any strong saturated colour. But to rule out the possibilities of decorating with red, or basing a colour scheme around it, is to miss the warmth and vitality that previous generations understood and heartily appreciated. Even quite small rooms can look wonderful in red, lending them a jewel-like intensity.

Red is a natural accent and for those who are incurably shy of making a bold statement, this may be the best way of learning to enjoy the colour. A red quilt, a splash of red in a tablecloth or as part of the sofa upholstery draws any room together successfully.

Pink is not light red but a colour in its own right. Where red is bold and brave, pink is delicate and soothing, a flattering warm colour in all its manifestations from the lightest rose-pink to shocking Schiaparelli. Very blue or cool pinks can sometimes look pasty, but in its subtle form, pink is unbeatably refined and beautifully luxurious.

EIGHTEENTH-CENTURY PANELLING PAINTED *SANG DE BOEUF* IS EVOCATIVE OF ANOTHER AGE.

WINTER RED

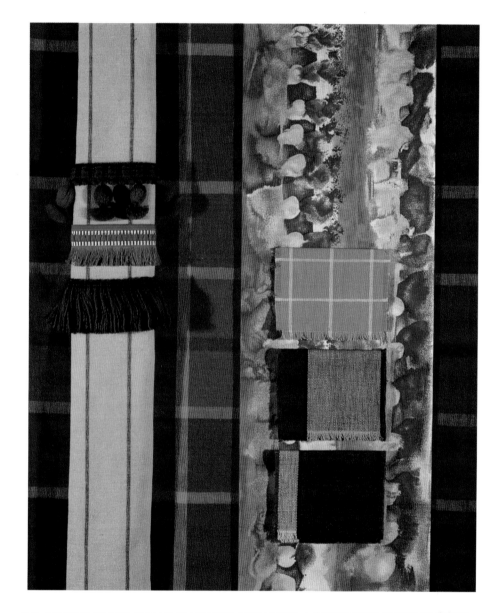

EYE-CATCHING CRIMSON IS WARMING AND LIVELY, A COLOUR TO CHEER UP COLD GREY WINTER DAYS. THIS EXUBERANTLY DRESSED BED, WITH ITS FLASH OF RED QUILT AND SIMPLE HANGINGS, WOULD BANISH THE CHILL. RED HAS ALWAYS FEATURED IN TRADITIONAL PATTERNS SUCH AS TARTANS, WHERE IT IS TYPICALLY COMBINED WITH DEEP FIR-GREEN AND A RICH WARM YELLOW. A REALLY VIVID CLEAR-RED, SUCH AS CRIMSON, IS AN EXCITING AND DEMANDING COLOUR. INTRODUCE LIMITED AREAS OF BRIGHT RED IN THE FORM OF A QUILT, TABLECLOTH, LAMPSHADE, PAINTED DOOR OR THROW: ITS ABILITY TO PRODUCE VITALITY IS SECOND TO NONE.

RED AND WHITE

WHITE DOMESTICATES RED, JUST AS IT ADDS A HOMELY QUALITY TO BLUES AND GREENS. RED-AND-WHITE CHECKED GINGHAM IS ALMOST SYNONYMOUS WITH HOSPITALITY; RED CHECKS, CALICO OR STRIPED FABRICS ARE COMMON IN EVERYDAY USE THROUGHOUT EUROPE AND AMERICA. THE FRESHNESS AND GAIETY OF RED AND WHITE MAKE AN IRRESISTIBLE COMBINATION, AS DISPLAYED BY THE RED PAINTED CASEMENT WINDOW IN THIS IRISH COTTAGE, FRAMING ROWS OF DAINTY LACE PANELS (LEFT). SOME RED-AND-WHITE COMBINATIONS ARE INHERENTLY MORE ELEGANT AND REFINED, SUCH AS THE CLASSIC *TOILE DE JOUY* PATTERN IN SOFT MADDER RED, A HINT OF WHICH IS IN THE DESIGN OF THIS PLATE (RIGHT).

EASTERN RED

CRIMSON AND GOLD CURTAINS GENERATE A MOOD OF ORIENTAL RICHNESS COMBINED WITH A FACING DRAPERY IN SWIRLING BURGUNDY PAISLEY. THE VICTORIANS WERE PARTICULARLY FOND OF STRONG, ENVELOPING REDS AND USED THEM TO GREAT EFFECT IN THEIR LAVISHLY FURNISHED ROOMS. ALL REDS LOOK WONDERFUL BY SOFT CANDLELIGHT OR FIRELIGHT, AND SUIT ROOMS THAT ARE USED FOR ENTERTAINING AND DINING. STRONG-TO DEEP-REDS OCCUR IN MANY EASTERN AND NEAR-EASTERN TEXTILES, IN KELIMS, CARPETS, PAISLEY FABRICS AND RICHLY EMBROIDERED HANGINGS. LAYERS OF THESE PATTERNS CAN BE BUILT UP EASILY AND NATURALLY, EACH COMPLEMENTING AND ECHOING THE OTHERS. AS IN ORIENTAL DESIGNS, BLUE-GREEN IS A GOOD PARTNER, BUT THE LIVELIEST ACCENT IS GOLD. TOUCHES OF GLITTER, IN A ROPE TIE-BACK, FRINGING, OR AS HERE, IN THE BOLD-STRIPED FABRIC ON A FOOTSTOOL, CATCH THE LIGHT AND ADD A RICH, GLOWING ATMOSPHERE.

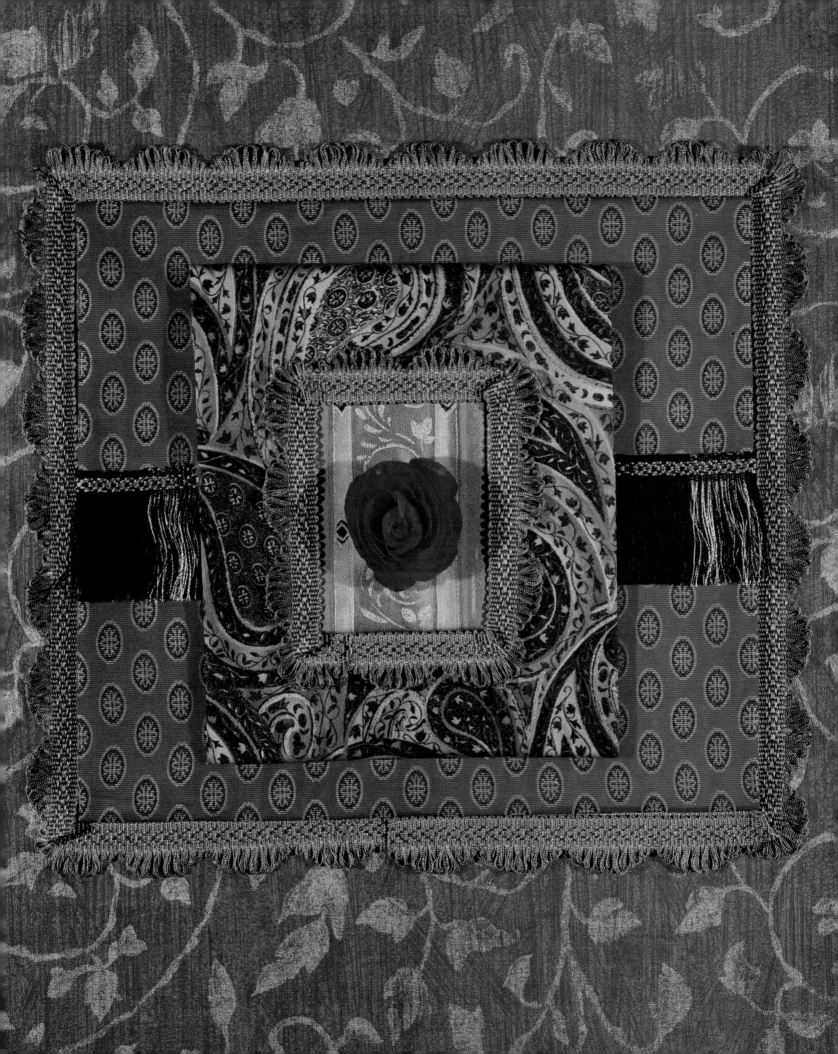

ELECTRIC RED

RED IS THE COLOUR IN THE SPECTRUM WHICH DRAWS
THE EYE THE MOST. SENSATIONAL EFFECTS CAN BE
CREATED BY SETTING RED WITH ITS COMPLEMENTARY
OR OPPOSITE AND REVELLING IN THE RESULTING
DYNAMISM. RED AND GREEN IN VARIOUS
COMBINATIONS VIBRATE; RED AND STRONG BLUE CAN
ALSO GENERATE GREAT COLOUR EXCITEMENT. MONET
DELIBERATELY JUXTAPOSED COMPLEMENTARIES: RED
POPPIES IN A GREEN FIELD. BRIGHT COLOUR HAS A
PRIMITIVE POWER AND ENERGY; IT IS THERE IN NATURE,
IN FLOWERS, LEAVES AND SEEDPODS AND IT IS PART OF
EVERY CULTURE. EVEN IF YOU DO NOT DECORATE YOUR
ENTIRE HOME IN BRILLIANT SHADES, YOU CAN BRING A
CORNER TO LIFE BY ASSEMBLING A COLOUR DISPLAY. A
BOWL OF FRUIT, A VASE OF FLOWERS, A COLLECTION
OF PLATES. THE INGREDIENTS COULD NOT BE SIMPLER
OR MORE ACCESSIBLE.

RICH RED

RED FOR LUXURY OR RICHNESS IS A TRADITIONAL ASSOCIATION, DATING FROM THE TIME WHEN RED SILK DAMASK WAS THE HEIGHT OF FURNISHING FASHION. YOU CAN BORROW AN ELEMENT OF THIS GRANDEUR BY ADDING RUBY-RED DETAILS SUCH AS CUSHIONS AND THROWS IN FINE FABRICS LIKE SATIN AND SILK (ABOVE LEFT AND RIGHT).

CUSHION COVERS ARE AN IDEAL WAY OF INTRODUCING COLOUR NOTES TO BRIGHTEN OR ENRICH A ROOM. AND BECAUSE THE AMOUNT OF FABRIC REQUIRED IS LIMITED, YOU CAN AFFORD TO BE MORE EXTRAVAGANT IN TERMS OF MATERIAL AND TRIMMING. THE WARM RICH-REDS WORK WELL WITH BUTTERCUP-YELLOWS AND GOLD (RIGHT).

PINK

PINK CAN BE AS PLAIN AS A PLASTERED WALL OR COLOURWASHED STUCCO, A ROBUST SHADE FOUND ON THE OUTSIDE OF HOUSES FROM TUSCANY TO PROVENCE TO SUFFOLK, ENGLAND (LEFT). PRETTY, DELICATE AND LUXURIOUS, PINK HAS ANOTHER MOOD, FOREVER ASSOCIATED WITH THE ROCOCO FANCIES OF MADAME DE POMPADOUR. STRAWBERRY SATIN, SHELL-STRIPED BROCADES AND FLORAL COTTONS ARE IRRESISTIBLE. FLATTERING, WARM AND ELEGANT, THIS IS THE CLASSIC COLOUR FOR A TRADITIONALLY FEMININE AND RESTFUL BEDROOM.

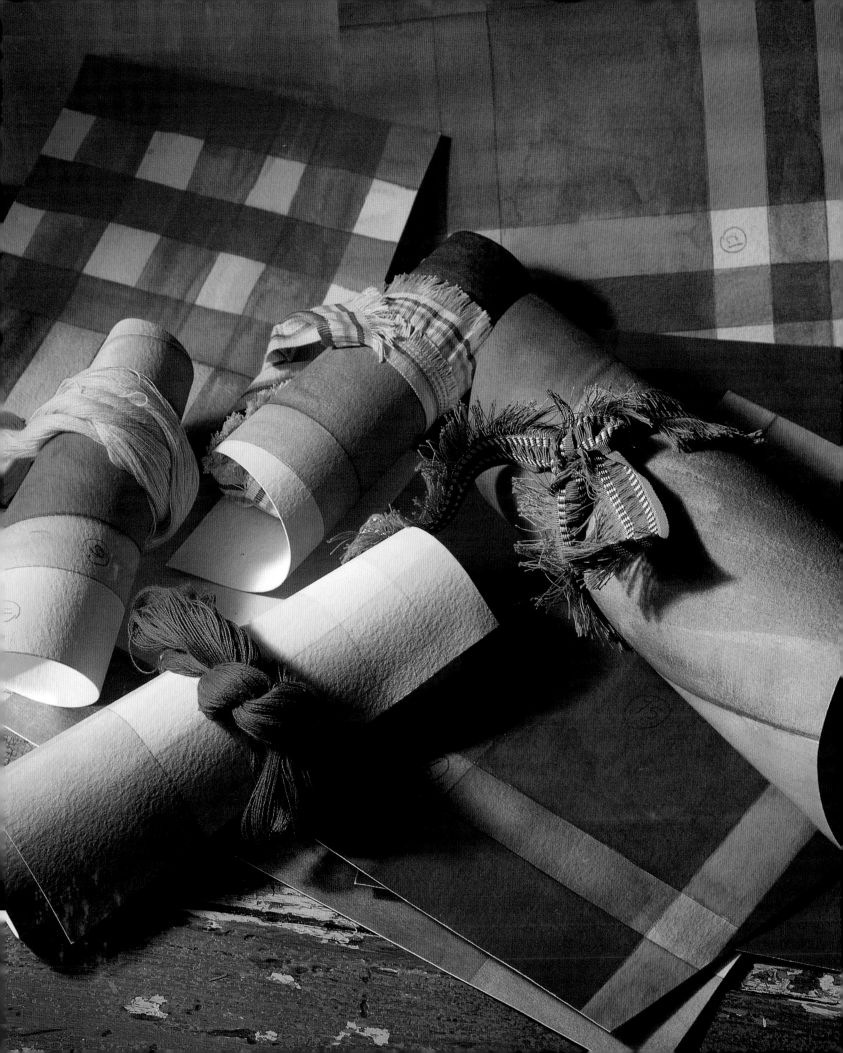

COLOUR PALETTES

'THIS TIME IT'S JUST SIMPLY MY BEDROOM, ONLY HERE
COLOUR IS TO DO EVERYTHING, AND GIVING BY ITS
SIMPLIFICATION A GRANDER STYLE TO THINGS, IS TO BE
SUGGESTIVE HERE OF *REST* OR OF SLEEP IN GENERAL. IN A
WORD, TO LOOK AT THE PICTURE OUGHT TO REST THE
BRAIN OR RATHER THE IMAGINATION.
THE WALLS ARE PALE VIOLET. THE FLOOR IS OF RED TILES.
THE WOOD OF THE BED AND CHAIRS IS THE YELLOW OF
FRESH BUTTER, THE SHEET AND PILLOWS VERY
LIGHT LEMON-GREEN.
THE COVERLET SCARLET. THE WINDOW GREEN.
THE TOILET TABLE ORANGE, THE BASIN BLUE.
THE DOORS LILAC.
AND THAT IS ALL – THERE IS NOTHING IN THIS ROOM
WITH CLOSED SHUTTERS.'

LETTER TO HIS BROTHER THEO,
VINCENT VAN GOGH

COLOUR PALETTES

THE FOLLOWING PAGES COMPRISE SEVEN DISTINCT COLOUR PALETTES BASED ON THE MAIN SECTIONS OF THE BOOK: WHITE, BLUE, GREEN, YELLOW, NATURAL, TERRACOTTA AND RED. EACH OFFERS A COLOUR FAMILY IN FABRIC AND WALLPAPERS SO YOU CAN SEE THE FULL RANGE AT A GLANCE AND DECIDE ON YOUR OWN PREFERENCES. IN ADDITION, FOUR

COLOUR SAMPLES HAVE BEEN CHOSEN WHICH REPRESENT COMPATIBLE OR COMPLEMENTARY SHADES TO EACH MAIN COLOUR, EACH GIVING INSPIRATION FOR A WIDER RICHER COLOUR PALETTE. THE ILLUSTRATION BELOW IS A KEY TO IDENTIFYING THE FABRIC AND WALLPAPER NAMES AND COLOURS THAT APPEAR IN THE PALETTES ON PAGES 173-185.

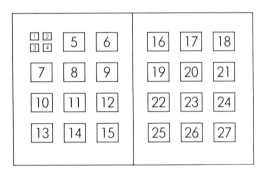

WHITE COLOUR PALETTE

1 DOUBLEGLAZE F38/15
2 FIREFLY F272/03
3 DOUBLEGLAZE F38/02
4 FIREFLY F272/53
5 FIREFLY F272/30
6 BANOL F180/05
7 SEDGE F261/08
8 MARQUETRY F258/01
9 KASAN F232/05
10 DAMAS FLEURI F131/08
11 RUSH F260/07
12 TIMUR F245/01
13 CASSIS F182/05
14 SIRSI F317/02
15 MANOSQUE F184/06
11 CASSIA F130/12
12 MANOSQUE F184/01
13 RUSH F260/08
14 MIREPOIX F183/01
15 SEDGE F261/09
16 BAKU P159/04
17 COLONNA P173/10
18 VIOTTOLO P174/08
19 STUCCO STRIPE P133/08
20 BAKU P159/27
21 PASSAGGIO P135/02
22 DOUBLEGLAZE F38/27
23 TANDA F321/01
24 THIZY F246/04
25 DEJEUNER SUR L'HERBE F251/01
26 DOUBLEGLAZE F38/28
27 AMBALA F318/03

BLUE COLOUR PALETTE

1 DOUBLEGLAZE F38/11
2 DOUBLEGLAZE F38/13
3 FIREFLY F272/59
4 SIRSI F317/09
5 TWINKLE TWINKLE P162/06
6 BAKU P159/06
7 CANDY STRIPE P140/02
8 STUCCO P10/21
9 STUCCO P10/22
10 DOUBLEGLAZE F38/26

GREEN COLOUR PALETTE

1 FIREFLY F272/67
2 FIREFLY F272/48
3 FIREFLY F272/53
4 DOUBLEGLAZE F38/41
5 DIAMANTE P136/05
6 STUCCO P10/10
7 MIANE P148/07
8 BAKU P159/01
9 PAGLIA P11/04

10 NANTUA F287/16
11 BIHAR F322/04
12 DOUBLEGLAZE F38/33
13 SEDGE F261/11
14 DOUBLEGLAZE F38/32
15 MARQUETRY F259/33
16 MIRANDOLA P146/03
17 PASSAGGIO P135/01
18 BAKU P159/05
19 SOLFERINO P145/09
20 MONTEBULLUNA P147/08
21 STUCCO P10/09
22 KASHGAR F233/05
23 SIRSI F317/08
24 DOUBLEGLAZE F38/30
25 RUSH F260/11
26 MANOSQUE F184/03
27 SEDGE F261/12

YELLOW COLOUR PALETTE

1 DOUBLEGLAZE F38/13
2 DOUBLEGLAZE F38/05
3 DOUBLEGLAZE F38/27
4 DOUBLEGLAZE F38/12
5 CANDY STRIPE P140/04
6 SOLFERINO P145/05
7 DOTTY P141/04
8 STUCCO P10/18
9 BAKU P159/15
10 FIREFLY F272/28
11 DOUBLEGLAZE F30/35
12 LAPALME F185/04
13 RUSH F260/06
14 FIREFLY F272/03
15 SEDGE F261/05
16 STUCCO F10/07
17 TWINKLE TWINKLE P162/03
18 STUCCO P10/18
19 TWINKLE TWINKLE P162/07
20 BAKU P159/13
21 PASSAGGIO P135/03
22 MIREPOIX F183/04
23 KASHGAR F233/01
24 LAPALISSE F286/10
25 NANTUA F287/17
26 DOUBLEGLAZE F38/39
27 RUSH F260/04

NATURAL COLOUR PALETTE

1 DOUBLEGLAZE F38/34
2 DOUBLEGLAZE F38/19
3 DOUBLEGLAZE F38/38
4 FIREFLY F272/18
5 PASSAGGIO P135/07
6 CASPIAN ROSE P154/05
7 BAKU P159/08
8 VIOTTOLO P174/04
9 HICKETY PICKETY P161/02
10 LICHEN P226/02
11 SEDGE F261/06
12 FIREFLY F272/36
13 SEDGE F261/07
14 LAPALISSE F286/03
15 MARQUETRY F258/12
16 TWINKLE TWINKLE P162/08
17 SOLFERINO P145/06
18 STUCCO P10/05

19 BAKU P159/10
20 MIRANDOLA P146/05
21 TAORMINA P150/21
22 FIREFLY F272/21
23 SEDGE F261/04
24 RUSH F260/13
25 THIZY F246/08
26 FIREFLY F272/24
27 TANDA F321/03

TERRACOTTA COLOUR PALETTE

1 DOUBLEGLAZE F38/41
2 FIREFLY F272/59
3 DOUBLEGLAZE F38/36
4 FIREFLY F272/07
5 DOTTY P141/03
6 BAKU P159/19
7 TWINKLE TWINKLE P162/05
8 LEAF FRESCO P13/06
9 BAKU P159/21
10 FIREFLY F272/13
11 SEDGE F261/03
12 DAMAS FLEURI F131/04
13 MANOSQUE F184/04
14 DOUBLEGLAZE F38/17
15 KASHGAR F233/04
16 STUCCO P10/17
17 STUCCO STRIPE P133/02
18 STUCCO P10/03
19 ASTRAKHAN P152/05
20 VIOTTOLO P174/07
21 PASSAGGIO P135/04
22 FIREFLY P272/19
23 LAPALISSE F286/06
24 SIRSI F317/04
25 LAPALME F185/03
26 OOTY F320/01
27 FIREFLY F272/17

RED COLOUR PALETTE

1 FIREFLY F272/30
2 DOUBLEGLAZE F38/27
3 FIREFLY F272/41
4 FIREFLY F272/01
5 FILIGRANA P138/01
6 CANDY STRIPE P140/06
7 TWINKLE TWINKLE P162/04
8 BAKU P159/22
9 DUSHAK P153/06
10 CROSSPATCH F194/07
11 FIREFLY F272/05
12 MARQUETRY F258/41
13 FIREFLY F272/06
14 MONTFERRAT F179/01
15 DOUBLEGLAZE F38/21
16 MONTEBULLUNA P147/04
17 ASTRAKHAN P152/07
18 STUCCO P010/04
19 STUCCO STRIPE P133/01
20 CARIOLA P015/01
21 PASSAGGIO P135/06
22 MIREPOIX F183/05
23 FIREFLY F272/07
24 ORISSA F314/03
25 LAPALISSE F286/05
26 THIZY F246/01
27 RUSH F260/02

WHITE COLOUR PALETTE

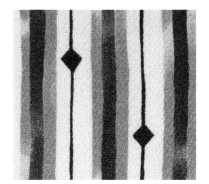
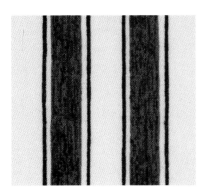

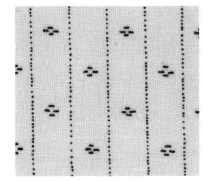

BLUE COLOUR PALETTE

GREEN COLOUR PALETTE

  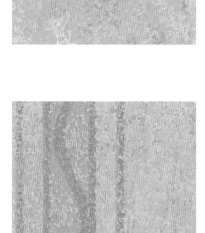

 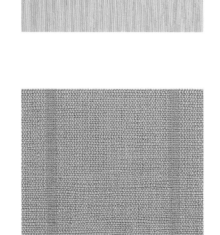 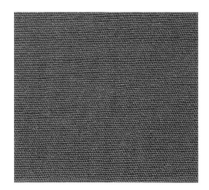

 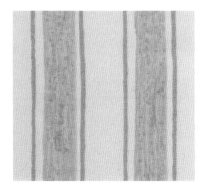 

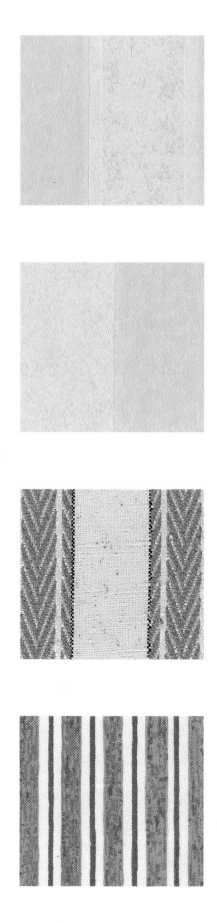

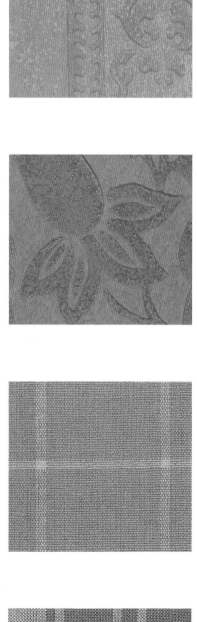

GREEN 177

YELLOW COLOUR PALETTE

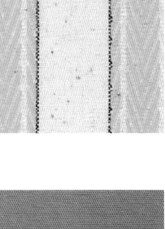

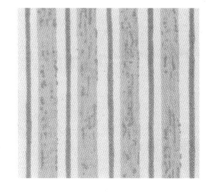

YELLOW 179

NATURAL COLOUR PALETTE

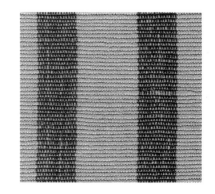

TERRACOTTA COLOUR PALETTE

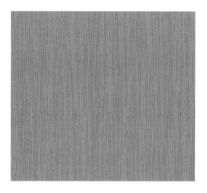

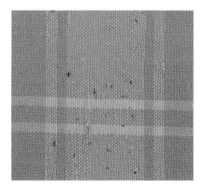

TERRACOTTA 183

RED COLOUR PALETTE

  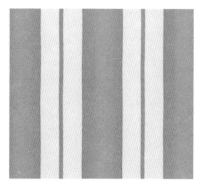

RED 185

FABRIC DIRECTORY

EACH OF THE FOLLOWING ILLUSTRATIONS IDENTIFIES THE DESIGNERS GUILD FABRICS FEATURED IN THE ROOM SETS THROUGHOUT THE BOOK.

FRENCH BLUE page 54

1 VIOTTOLO P174/08
2 CHIMU T8/05
3 SEERSUCKER T11/05
4 TUFTS T13/05
5 RIVOLO F274/02
6 PUNTASPILLE F275/02
7 THIZY F246/04
8 PERGAMENA F276/03

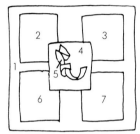

ITALIAN CHECK page 65

1 COCHIN F316/04
2 AMBALA F318/03
3 MYSORE F315/05
4 SIRSI F317/05
5 OCONA T23/01
6 SIRSI F317/10
7 TANDA F321/01

GARDEN page 84

1 SIRSI F317/08
2 THE MELON PATCH F312/03
3 OOTY F320/03
4 ORISSA F314/05
5 ORISSA F314/04
6 OCONA T23/02
7 HARVEST F313/04
8 MYSORE F315/04
9 OCONA T23/06

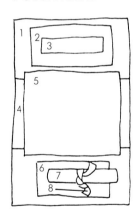

WHITE LIGHT page 40

1 NANTUA F287/01
2 SEERSUCKER T11/07
3 DAMAS FLEURI F131/08
4 HOPSACK F330/01
5 DOUBLEGLAZE F38/01

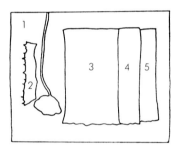

PISTACHIO page 80

1 BAKU P159/01
2 ORISSA F314/01
3 ARANI F319/04
4 BIHAR F322/04
5 SIRSI F317/08
6 MANOSQUE F184/06
7 SIRSI F317/09
8 OCONA F323/03

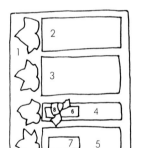

APPLE GREEN page 88

1 COLONNA P173/06
2 KASAN F232/03
3 CHAZELLE F240/01
4 NELL O'RTO P175/01
5 GHIRLANDA F280/01
6 NANTUA F287/16
7 PASSARIANO F204/05
8 OCONA T23/03

CLASSICAL STRIPE page 45

1 SIRSI F317/06
2 THIZY F246/07
3 SEDGE F261/08
4 OCONA T23/03
5 PROVENCE F174/02
6 LA VERDIERE F176/02
7 MANOSQUE F184/06
8 LAPALME F185/06
9 CASTELLANE F186/05

CHECKS AND SPOTS page 59

1 CASTELLANE F186/01
2 JALNA F325/07
3 MIREPOIX F183/02
4 SIRSI F317/03
5 BIHAR F322/05
6 BANDRA F324/01
7 MANOSQUE F184/01
8 LA VERDIERE F176/01
9 SEDGE F261/09

CHROME YELLOW page 102

1 NANTUA F287/18
2 NANTUA F287/15
3 NANTUA F287/04
4 TUFTS T19/02
5 ORION T18/02
6 HUARI T22/05
7 HUARI T22/04

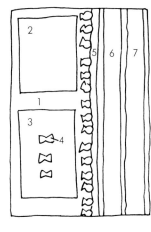

GOLD page 106

1 CHIMU T08/03
2 CHAZELLE F240/03
3 NELL O'RTO F279/02
4 ASIAGO F205/01
5 NANTUA F287/17
6 GIVORS F239/01
7 THIZY F246/05

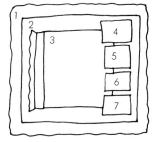

TUSCAN GLOW page 114

For diagram, see CHECKS
AND SPOTS, opposite.

1 JALNA F325/05
2 OOTY F320/02
3 JALNA F325/02
4 VITA F323/01
5 SUKMA F326/01
6 TANDA F321/02
7 COCHIN F316/02
8 BANDRA F324/02
9 JALNA F325/06

DRIFTWOOD page 127

1 SIRSI F317/01
2 COCHIN F316/03
3 TRACER F294/03
4 LEAFLIGHT F295/03
5 ARIANI F319/03
6 TANDA F321/03
7 CHIMU T08/07
8 TUFT T13/07

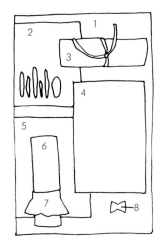

FRESCO page 130

1 TORCELLO P150/01
2 MIRANDOLA P146/02
3 SOLFERINO P145/01
4 BAKU P159/09
5 STUCCO P10/15
6 MANDRIA P151/02
7 CARIOLA P15/07

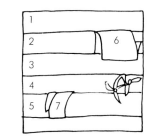

CORAL page 140

1 STUCCO P10/03
2 COCHIN F316/01
3 CHIMU T08/02
4 DOUBLEGLAZE F38/01
5 CORAL T10/02
6 SIRSI F317/06
7 SIRSI F317/04
8 ORISSA F314/02
9 BIHAR F322/04

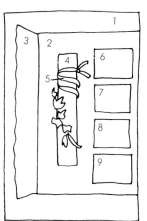

SPICE page 144
From top to bottom:

1 NANTUA F287/19
2 MYSORE F315/03
3 LAPALISSE F286/06
4 ARANI F319/02

MADRAS page 148

1 OOTY F320/01
2 HARVEST F313/01
3 SEERSUCKER T11/02
4 THE MELON PATCH F312/01
5 AURICULA F288/01
6 BIHAR F322/06
7 ONION T8/04

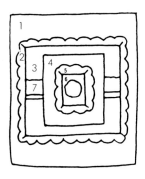

WINTER RED page 159

1 ORISSA F314/03
2 RUCHE T16/04
3 BIHAR F322/01
4 SIRSI F317/08
5 AMBALA F318/01
6 AMBALA F318/02
7 ONION T18/04
8 OCONA T23/01

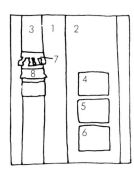

EASTERN RED page 163

1 TIMUR F245/04
2 FAN EDGE T4/04
3 THIZY F246/01
4 ASTRAKHAN F242/05
5 FAN EDGE T4/04
6 BOKHARA F244/05
7 TUMBEZ T3/05

DESIGNERS GUILD STOCKISTS

Designers Guild fabrics are available from their London showrooms at 271 and 277 Kings Road, London SW3 5EN.
Telephone: 020 7351 5775, and through a comprehensive network of stockists which include those listed below.

AVON

Bristol Guild, 68-70 Park Street, Bristol, BS1 5JY.
0117 926 5548

Michael Bracey Interiors, 30 The Mall, Clifton, Bristol, BS8 4DS. 0117 973 4664

Michael Jefferies Design, 3 Upper Lambridge Street, Larkhall, Bath BA1 6RY.
01225 310417

BUCKINGHAMSHIRE

Morgan Gilder Furniture 83 High Street, Stony Stratford, Milton Keynes MK11 1AT. 01908 568674

CAMBRIDGESHIRE

At Home, 44 Newnham Road, Cambridge CB3 9EY.
01223 321283

CHANNEL ISLANDS

The Designers' Choice, 21 Seale Street, St Helier, Jersey, JE2 3QG.
01534 24678

CHESHIRE

Designers, 15 London Road, Alderley Edge, Cheshire, SK9 7UT. 01625 586851

DEVON

G&H Interiors, 1 The Old Pannier Market, High Street, Honiton, EX14 8LS.
01404 42063

DORSET

Individual Interior Design, 58-60 Poole Road, Westbourne, Bournemouth, BH4 9DZ. 01202 763256

EIRE

O'Mahoney Interiors, Enniskeane, West Cork.
023 47123

Cotton Box Interiors, 21 Middle Street, Galway.
091 564373

Geraldine Hudson Interior Furnishings, 18 Herbert Lane, Dublin 2. 660 0325

J Lyons Interiors, The Square, Castlerea, Co. Roscommon.
0907 20339

ESSEX

Clement Joscelyne Ltd, 9-11 High Street, Brentwood, CM14 4RG. 01277 225420

Devon House Interiors, 3-4 Devon House, Hermon Hill, Wanstead, Essex, E11 2AW.
020 8518 8112

GLOUCESTERSHIRE

Upstairs Downstairs, 19 Rotunda Terrace, Montpellier Street, Cheltenham, GL50 1SW. 01242 514023

HAMPSHIRE

The Interior Trading Company, 578 Marmion Road, Southsea, PO5 2AT. 01705 838038

HEREFORDSHIRE & WORCESTERSHIRE

Cloud Nine Interiors, 12 St. Andrews Street, Droitwich, WR9 8DY.
01905 779988

HERTFORDSHIRE

Clement Joscelyne Ltd, Market Square, Bishops Stortford, CM23 3XA.
01279 506731

David Lister Interiors, 6 Leyton Road, Harpenden, AL5 2TL. 01582 764270

KENT

John Thornton Interiors, 43 St. Peter's Street, Canterbury, CT1 2BG. 01227 785284

Kotiki Interiors, 22-24 Grove Hill Road, Royal Tunbridge Wells, TN1 1RZ.
01892 521369

Mary Ensor Interiors, 13 Crescent Road, Tunbridge Wells, TN1 2LU.
01892 523003

LANCASHIRE

John Thompson Design Centre, 328-336 Church Street, Blackpool, FY1 3QH.
01253 302515

LEICESTERSHIRE

Harlequin Interiors, 11 Laseby Lane, Leicester, LE1 5DR.
01162 620994

LINCOLNSHIRE

Pilgrim Décor, 35 Wide Bargate, Boston, PE21 6SR.
01205 363917

LONDON

Designers Guild, 271 and 277 Kings Road, SW3 5EN.
020 7351 5775

Harrods, Knightsbridge, SW1.
020 7730 1234

Heal & Son, 196 Tottenham Court Road, W1P 9LD.
020 7636 1666

Liberty, Regent Street, W1.
020 7734 1234

Interiors of Chiswick, 4540458 Chiswick High Road, London, W4 5TT.
020 8994 0073

NORFOLK

Clement Joscelyne Ltd, The Granary, 5 Bedford Street, Norwich, NR2 1AL.
01603 623220

NORTHAMPTONSHIRE

Clasix Design & Development Ltd, Billing Wharf, Cogenhoe, Northampton NN7 1NH.
01604 891333

NORTHERN IRELAND

Fultons Fine Furnishings, Hawthorne House, Boucher Crescent, Belfast, BT12 6HU.
01232 382168

NOTTINGHAMSHIRE

Lillie Interiors, 16 London Road, Newark, NG24 1TW.
01636 705693

SCOTLAND

Cairns Interiors, 1110-113 High Street, Old Aberdeen, AB2 3EN. 01224 487490

Mary Maxwell Designs, 63 Dublin Street, Edinburgh, EH3 6NS. 0131 557 2173

SOMERSET

The Curtain Pole, 64 High Street, Glastonbury, Somerset, BA6 9DY.
01458 831 466

STAFFORDSHIRE

Ann Clarke Design Ltd, 36 Tamworth Street, Lichfield, WS13 6JJ. 01543 416366

SUFFOLK

Edwards of Hadleigh, 53 High Street, Hadleigh, IP7 5AB. 01473 827271

Clement Joscelyne Ltd, 16 Langton Place, Bury St. Edmunds, IP33 1NE.
01284 753824

SURREY

Design Studio, 39 High Street, Reigate, RH2 9AE.
01737 248228

Homeflair, 26 Queens Road, Kingston-Upon-Thames, KT2 7SN. 020 8546 2033

Interior Motives, 151 Shirley Road, Croydon, CR0 8SS.
020 8654 2776

Pipeline-in-Dec of Cobham, 8 Postboys Row, Between Streets, Cobham, KT11 1AB.
01932 862764

SUSSEX

The Design House, 56A High Street, Steyning, West Sussex, BN44 3RD. 01903 812845

TYNE AND WEAR

Abercrombies, 140-142 Manor House Road, Jesmond, Newcastle Upon Tyne, NE2 2NA.
0191 281 7182

Roy Errington (WB) Ltd, 6 Cauldwell Lane, Monkseaton, Whitley Bay, NE25 8LN.
0191 252 7316

WALES

Country Interiors, Goat Street, Haverfordwest, Pembrokeshire, SA61 1PX.
01437 768217

Maskreys, 116-120 Whitchurch Road, Cardiff, CF4 3YL.
01222 229371

YORKSHIRE

Plaskitt & Plaskitt 8A Walmgate, York, YO1 2TJ.
01904 624670

AUSTRALIA

Wardlow Pty Ltd, 230-232 Auburn Road, Hawthorn, 3122 Melbourne, Victoria.
61 3819 4233/882 7256

DENMARK

Designers Guild Denmark, Bukkeballevej 24, 2960 Rungsted Kyst.
00 45 42 864 480

GREECE

Persefone n Diamandas & Co. EE, 49 Anagnostopoulou Street, GR-106 73 Athens.
00 301 360 9324

NEW ZEALAND

Mokum Textiles Lt, 11 Cheshire Street, Parnell, Auckland1.
64 9 379 3041

NORWAY

Design Works, PO Box 5019, Majorsteun 0301, Oslo 3.
00 47 2 465 641

SOUTH AFRICA

HF Home Fabrics Ltd, 60 Old Pretoria Road, Halfway House, Midrand 1685, Johannesburg.
00 27 11 805 0300

SWEDEN

Tapi, Kommendörsgatan 22, 114 48, Stockholm.
00 46 8 661 0380

SWITZERLAND

Isabelle Turzi, 10 rue Michel Chauvet, 1208 Geneva.
00 41 22 346 3201

ACKNOWLEDGMENTS

The publisher thanks the following photographers and organizations for their kind permission to reproduce the photographs in this book:
5 above centre Dominic Sansoni/Impact Photos; 5 above right Carlos Navajas; 5 centre left Carlos Navajas; 5 centre Tim Woodcock/TWP; 5 below left Jean-Pierre Godeaut; 5 below centre Ian A Griffiths/Robert Harding; 8-9 James Morris; 10 below left Patricia Aithie/Ffotograff; 17 Paul Forster/Impact Photos; 19 The Tate Gallery, London (courtesy of Howard Hodgkin); 27 below and centre David Montgomery/Conran Octopus; 28 above Jean-Pierre Godeaut; 28 below Christian Sarramon; 29 Christopher Rennie/Robert Harding; 30 David Montgomery/Conran Octopus; 32-3 Carlos Navajas; 35 above left Carlos Navajas; 35 above right Patricia Aithie/Ffotograff; 35 below left Carlos Navajas; 35 below right Dominic Sansoni/Impact Photos; 38-9 Jean-Pierre Godeaut (Catherine Margaretis); 42 left Elizabeth Whiting and Associates/Cassell; 42 right La Maison de Marie Claire/Snitt/Bayle; 43 Elizabeth Whiting and Associates/Cassell; 46-7 Laurence Delderfield; 49 above left Christian Sarramon; 49 above right S & O Mathews; 49 below left Carlos Navajas; 49 below right Patricia Aithie/Ffotograff; 52-3 Guy Bouchet; 56 Elizabeth Whiting and Associates/Cassell; 57 Elizabeth Whiting and Associates/Cassell; 60 above Nedra Westwater/Robert Harding; 61 above right Peter Moszynski/The Hutchison Library; 61 below left Carlos Navajas; 62 right Robin Guild; 63 Christian Sarramon; 67 below left Laurence Delderfield; 68-9 Carlos Navajas; 71 above left Richard Bryant/Arcaid (courtesy of the Mount Vernon Ladies Association); 71 above right Robin Guild; 71 below left David Montgomery/Conran Octopus; 72-3 Schuster/Robert Harding; 75 above left Carlos Navajas; 75 below left Mark Cator/Impact Photos; 75 below right Jacqui Hurst; 78-9 La Maison de Marie Claire/Bailache/Rozensztroch; 86 Mike England; 87 Christian Sarramon; 92 below Laurence Delderfield; 93 Guy Bouchet; 94-5 Steve Bavister/Robert Harding; 97 above left Ken Gillham/Robert Harding; 97 above right Tim Woodcock/TWP; 97 below left Philippe Perdereau; 97 below right Christian Sarramon; 101 Guy Bouchet; 104 Jacqui Hurst; 105 Michael Boys/Boys Syndication; 109 Richard Bryant/Arcaid (Homewood House); 110 Christian Sarramon; 112 below Guy Bouchet; 112-3 above Steven Moore/Impact Photos; 116 Dominic Sansoni/Impact Photos; 117 Tom Woodcock/TWP; 118-9 Martin Black/Impact Photos; 121 above left Jacqui Hurst; 121 above right Peter Ryan/Robert Harding; 121 below left Carlos Navajas; 125 Jean-Pierre Godeaut; 128 above Carlos Navajas; 129 above right Tim Woodcock/TWP; 129 below left Walter Rawlings/Robert Harding; 135 above left Jean-Pierre Godeaut; 135 above right Christian Sarramon; 135 below left Robin Guild; 135 below right Liba Taylor/The Hutchison Library; 138-9 La Maison de Marie Claire/Beaufre/Billaud; 146 below Jean-Pierre Godeaut; 147 above left Guy Bouchet; 150-1 Robert Dowling/Robert Harding; 153 above left Ian A Griffiths/Robert Harding; 153 above right Tim Woodcock/TWP; 153 below left Tim Woodcock/TWP; 153 below right Jacqui Hurst; 156-7 The World of Interiors/Tim Beddow; 160 Robert Francis/The Hutchison Library; 164 above S & O Mathews; 165 above right Jesco Von Puttkamer/The Hutchison Library; 165 below left Christian Sarramon; 168 Christian Sarramon.

The following photographs were specially taken by David Montgomery for Designers Guild: 1-4, 5 above left, 6, 10 above and centre, 10 below right, 12-3, 14, 15, 16, 20, 21, 23, 26, 27 above, 31, 36-7, 41, 44, 50-1, 55, 58, 60 below, 61 above left, 61 below right, 62 left, 64-5, 66, 67 above, 67 below left, 70, 71 below right, 76-7, 80-1, 82-5, 89, 90, 91, 92 above, 98-9, 103, 107, 108, 111, 112 above, 112-3 below, 113, 114, 122-3, 126, 128 below, 129 above left, 129 below right, 130-1, 132-3, 136-7, 141, 142-3, 144-5, 146 above, 147 above right, 147 below, 149, 154-5, 158-9, 161, 162, 164 below, 165 above left, 165 below right, 166-7, 169, 170, 189, 192.

The publisher would like to thank Harper Collins Publishers for their kind permission to reproduce extracts from *The Letters of Vincent Van Gogh* on pages 11, 118 and 171.

INDEX